Library of
Davidson College

TWAYNE'S WORLD AUTHORS SERIES
A Survey of the World's Literature

Sylvia Bowman, Indiana University
GENERAL EDITOR

SPAIN

Gerald Wade, Vanderbilt University
Janet W. Díaz, University of North Carolina

EDITORS

Francisco Delicado

TWAS 335

FRANCISCO DELICADO

By BRUNO M. DAMIANI
The Catholic University of America

Twayne Publishers, Inc. :: New York

Copyright © 1974 by Twayne Publishers, Inc.
All Rights Reserved

Library of Congress Cataloging in Publication Data
Damiani, Bruno.
　Francisco Delicado.

　(Twayne's world authors series, TWAS 335. Spain)
Bibliography: p. 143.
　1. Delicado, Francisco, 16th cent.
PQ6388.D2Z63　　　863'.3　　　74-13041
ISBN 0-8057-2265-3

MANUFACTURED IN THE UNITED STATES OF AMERICA

TO
ALESSANDRO CRISAFULLI

Contents

About the Author
Preface
1. Delicado: Life and Works — 13
2. General Considerations on Portrait of Lozana:
   The Exuberant Andalusian Woman — 18
3. Influences on *Lozana* — 25
4. Delicado's Role in *Lozana* — 40
5. Historicity of *Lozana* — 47
6. Meaning and Form of *Lozana* — 62
7. Picaresque Characteristics of *Lozana* — 92
8. *El modo de adoperare el legno de India occidentale*
   (On the Use of the West Indies' Wood) — 103
9. Delicado and Aretino: Aspects of a Literary Profile — 110
10. Summation — 119
    Notes and References — 123
    Selected Bibliography — 143
    Index — 149

About the Author

Bruno M. Damiani is Associate Professor of Romance Languages and Literature at The Catholic University of America. He holds a B.A. and an M.A. degree from Ohio State University and a Ph.D. from Johns Hopkins University. He has received research and travel grants from the American Philosophical Society, the American Council of Learned Societies, and Catholic University.

Professor Damiani has published an edition of *Lozana* (Madrid: Castalia, 1969), and of *Celestina* (Madrid: Cátedra, 1974), and numerous articles on Spanish and comparative literature in the *Boletín de la Real Academia Española, Revista Hispánica Moderna, Modern Language Notes,* and other scholarly journals. Castalia is soon to publish his edition of *La pícara Justina.* He has served as academic consultant for the Department of Health, Education, and Welfare, and he is currently on the Board of Directors of the *Quaderni Ibero-Americani.*

Preface

In recent years Francisco Delicado has finally been recognized as a significant writer of the Spanish Renaissance. Several important studies of his *Retrato de la Lozana andaluza* (Portrait of Lozana: The Exuberant Andalusian Woman) attest to a new interest in the novel as a masterpiece of realistic literature. With the recognition of Delicado's literary talents, critics have paid more attention to his art and less to the particular episodes of his or his protagonists' libertine life. Through this study of Delicado and of his novelistic art, I hope to further this new appreciation of the writer and his work.

In chapter 1, I present the few biographical and bibliographical facts known about Delicado. To facilitate reference and to place the work in its proper artistic and historical perspective, in chapter 2 I offer some general considerations of the plot, structure, and criticism of *Lozana*. In chapter 3, where I cite the literary influences on the novel, I show that *Lozana* is not an isolated product of Spanish literature with no literary antecedents as some scholars have maintained. Since one of the most interesting features of *Lozana* is the author's intervention in the work, as a friend and confidant of the protagonist, I analyze the significance of Delicado as author and character in chapter 4. Such intervention is not only literary, but also of biographical, importance, because it sheds light on the life of the author.

Lozana purports to be a literary portrait of Renaissance Rome; as such, it possesses a very notable historical background. This I discuss in chapter 5. However, the novel is not a mere historical chronicle; it is a work of art, and this I try to make evident in chapter 6, which deals with the meaning and form of *Lozana*. In chapter 7 I point out the affinity between *Lozana* and the picaresque novel. This chapter reinforces the belief that Delicado's work has a very meaningful relationship with the literary tradition of Spain. In chapter 8 I study

Delicado's treatise on venereal disease, *El modo de adoperare el legno de India occidentale* (On the Use of the West Indies' Wood). In a papal proclamation, Clement VII praised the work for its humanitarian value. Furthermore, the treatise is important not only for the history of medicine, but also as a source of the author's biography and as a document of humanistic writing. In chapter 9 I provide a comparative study of Delicado and Aretino, a contemporary of the Spanish writer and an equally keen painter of the social condition of the time.

An integral part of Delicado's artistry consists of his masterly use of lively, spontaneous, colloquial, and plastic language. To show the vividness and charm of his style, it has been desirable, at times, to provide fragments of the original Spanish, Italian, Portuguese, and Catalan texts. The translations that accompany those passages are my own; they try to reflect some of the flavor if not the vigor and charm of the original.

Because of the relatively limited number of studies that have been made on Delicado, I have attempted to provide a comprehensive bibliography which could be useful to the student who may wish to do further research on Delicado. The bibliography is divided into three categories: the works of Delicado, the editions of *Lozana,* and the studies on Delicado and his works. I have accompanied most items with a brief explanatory note.

Finally, I should like to express my thanks to the American Philosophical Society and The Catholic University of America for grants that have facilitated my research here and in Europe. Portions of this book have appeared in slightly different form in *Modern Language Notes, Quaderni Ibero-Americani,* and *Kentucky Romance Quarterly.* I am deeply grateful to the editors of these journals and to the Johns Hopkins Press for their kind permission to reprint them.

It is with gratitude that I acknowledge my indebtedness to Professor Elias Rivers, who introduced me to Delicado and to the Spanish Renaissance. I should like to express my appreciation to Professors Bruce Wardropper, Antonio Vilanova, and José Hernández Ortiz, whose studies on Delicado have been truly revealing and inspiring. To Professor Francisco Márquez Villanueva I owe my sincere thanks for sending me a prepublication copy of his article on "The conversos in the *Lozana"* and for his critical suggestions on chapter 6.

Special acknowledgment is due to Professor Alessandro Crisafulli,

Preface

who has scrutinized my typescript with his knowledgeable and intelligent eye, and who has provided valuable advice for the improvement of the text. To the Reverend Father Robert Trisco I owe thanks for certain editorial suggestions. I should also like to thank Professor Gerald E. Wade for offering me the opportunity of making available to English readers this first book on Francisco Delicado. Last but not least, I wish to thank my wife for her unceasing support, and for her assistance in gathering library material, typing, and proofreading.

BRUNO M. DAMIANI

Washington, D. C.

CHAPTER 1

Francisco Delicado: Life and Works

I *Birth, Family, and Education*

OF Francisco Delicado, whose original surname was probably Delgado, we lack the extensive biographical sketches available for most other sixteenth-century writers. Actually, the little we know about him comes from what he himself tells us in his works. From textual information we may deduce that Delicado was born about 1480, in the vicinity of Cordova (XLVII, 187 - 189).[1] It appears, however, that early in life his family moved to the town of Martos, in the province of Jaén, a place apparently well-known to him, and for which he displays a notable sentimental attachment. From the evidence at hand there is good indication that Delicado and his family were originally Jews who later became *conversos* (converts to Christianity), a likelihood made plausible by his profound knowledge of their life and customs (VI - XI, 47 - 61).[2]

Concerning Delicado's education, the only facts available are, first, that he studied for the priesthood, received Holy Orders, and was subsequently given the vicarship of Martos; and, second, that he considered himself a disciple of the humanist Antonio de Nebrija (XIV, 77). It may indeed be possible that Delicado sought inspiration in Nebrija, the father of Spanish philology, a classicist, biblical scholar, and an exponent of Renaissance individualism. Delicado, like his teacher, shows a significant knowledge of classical letters, scriptural material, and contemporary linguistic and literary currents; he also displays a keen awareness of social problems. His own intellectual activity reflects a wide range of interests: novelistic, editorial, and scientific.

II *Delicado in Rome*

As a possible result of Inquisitorial practices against a great number of converts and of the Expulsion Edict of 1492, which sent the Jews of Spain into exile, Delicado joined the massive exodus of many of his compatriots to Italy and established himself in Rome, where he remained until 1528. It has also been suggested that Delicado's move to Rome was prompted by his desire to seek a benefice; this he obtained as vicar of Valle de Cabezuela, a village in the province of Cáceres. Evidently, this benefice did not require him to reside in Spain, since it does not appear that he left Italy during that time.

Delicado's years in Italy concur with the height of Italo-Hispanic relations in the Renaissance. Spain's presence as a commercial and cultural force had progressively increased from the time King Alfonso of Aragon moved the seat of his kingdom to Naples, in the fifteenth century. By the beginning of the sixteenth century, such Spanish romances of chivalry and sentimental novels as the *Amadís de Gaula* (Amadís of Gaul) and the *Cárcel de amor* (Prison of Love) were read with enthusiasm by distinguished Italian writers and courtly figures, among them Torquato Tasso and Isabella d'Este; the dramatists Juan del Encina and Torres Naharro presented their plays in Castilian at Rome, where another Spaniard, Juan de Torquemada, the famous theologian, taught canon law for twenty years;[3] the throne of Saint Peter was occupied by a Spanish pontiff, Rodrigo Borja (Alexander VI), whose court flourished with Spanish prelates and intellectuals. It is indeed possible that during his stay in Rome Delicado became acquainted with some of his compatriots and very likely frequented their social circles and was aware of their artistic activities.[4] In this cultural and intellectual milieu Delicado nourished his Spanish interests and assimilated many of the Italian humanistic currents.

Delicado, however, must have known not only the refined world of the arts but also the mundane quarters of the charlatans, the pimps, and the courtesans. In fact, it is in the course of his intimate association with the latter that he became a victim of venereal disease, an infirmity which afflicted him for twenty-three years (1503 - 1526), many of which he spent at the Hospital St. James, in Rome. As a result of his personal experiences with that long and dreadful disease, Delicado wrote two medical treatises: *De consolatione infirmorum* (On Consoling the Infirm, Rome, 1525?) and *El modo de adoperare el legno de India occidentale* (On the Use of the West Indies' Wood). Of these, the first is now lost, and the second, published in Rome, in 1525, is known only through a later edition which appeared in Venice in 1529. It is a work which deals with the therapeutic proper-

Delicado: Life and Works

ties of the *guayaco* ("guaiacum wood"), which had been used by the indigenous inhabitants of the West Indies to cure a variety of diseases. The early explorers of the New World, realizing the beneficial qualities of this medicinal plant, took it to Europe where it became a leading remedy for the cure of syphilis. The particulars of Delicado's treatise on the guaiacum and its historical and medical importance are discussed in chapter 8 of this book.

While in Rome, Delicado also wrote a handbook for clerics, *Spechio vulgare per li sacerdoti che administraranno li sacramenti in ciascheduna parrochia* (A Vernacular Manual for Those Priests Who Will Administer the Sacraments in Each Parish), now lost.[5] In addition, during his years in Rome Delicado composed most of his novel, the *Retrato de la Lozana andaluza* (Portrait of Lozana: The Exuberant Andalusian Woman), which was published in Venice, in 1528.

III *Delicado in Venice*

On February 10, 1528, nine months after Spanish and German troops had stormed and sacked Rome, Delicado left the Eternal City. For fear of reprisal from the local population, Delicado, along with many other Spaniards, sought refuge in Venice, a city hospitable to foreigners and friendly to literary men. There Delicado met Andrea Navagero, the Venetian ambassador to Spain. The contact with the ambassador provided Delicado with some very interesting and recently discovered archaeological information about Martos, the latter's adopted hometown.[6] It is very possible that Navagero, himself a man of letters and a respected humanist, introduced Delicado to Nicolini da Sabio, one of the most distinguished printers of the time.

Although the Adriatic capital had been one of the Italian cities in which Spanish influence was felt the least, it did become, in the sixteenth century, a major center for the diffusion of Spanish letters.[7] This was largely due to its flourishing printing industry, which attracted to Venice skilled printers from various regions of Italy. To many of those typographers, the printing of Spanish books seemed a very logical and worthwhile enterprise, especially since the Spanish language enjoyed a considerable popularity among all the social classes. The demand for the printing of Spanish books in sixteenth century Venice is reflected by the publication of a number of well-known works; among these, the *Cárcel de amor* (Prison of Love), *Cuestión de amor* (Question of Love), and the poetry of Juan

Boscán.[8] In these very propitious surroundings Delicado continued his literary career, first by completing and publishing his *Portrait of Lozana: The Exuberant Andalusian Woman,* then by sending to press the second and only extant edition of *On the Use of the West Indies' Wood,* and finally by becoming an editor of Spanish books.

IV Delicado's Editorial Activity

It was a common practice among sixteenth-century Venetian printers to avail themselves of the services of Spanish citizens to translate, revise, or edit Spanish books.[9] Having acquired a certain literary reputation from the publication of his earlier works, Delicado became increasingly sought-after for such editorial assistance. Thus, we find him involved in the preparation of various editions, which include the *Tragicomedia de Calisto y Melibea* (Tragicomedy of Calixtus and Melibea), known as *Celestina* (1531); *Amadís of Gaul* (1533); and *Los tres libros del caballero Primaleón et Polendos su hermano* (The Three Books of the Knight Primaleón and of Polendos, His Brother, 1534). The texts of these editions are reproduced with substantial faithfulness to the originals, and the print is sufficiently clear and correct. Delicado humbly notes that his role in the preparation of these editions is limited to the correction of printing errors, although we know his contribution was somewhat more substantial. The *Amadís* edition contains corrections that are, at times, gratuitous, and Delicado replaces the original prologue with his own; on the other hand, his edition of *Primaleón* is scrupulously done, as seen from the fact he not only based his text on the first printing of the work but also interjected certain significant emendations, all of which reflects a good critical ability.[10] In general, it appears Delicado possessed a reasonably good knowledge of Spanish philology and phonetics at a time when the formal study of language sounds was still in a primitive stage. A good example of his knowledge of linguistic matters is the essay on comparative Italo-Hispanic pronunciation, which he includes in his editions of *Celestina* and *Primaleón.* This composition, entitled *Introducción que muestra el Delicado a pronunciar la lengua española* (Introduction Which Delicado Offers on the Pronunciation of the Spanish Language) is a document of "bilingual didacticism,"[11] in which Delicado discusses the consonantal discrepancies between Spanish and Italian and provides rules for pronunciation. In many respects, his discussion of certain consonantal sounds has been considered an important contribution that reinforces the linguistic studies made in the earlier part of the sixteenth century by the Italian Gian Giorgio Trissino.[12]

The pedagogic introduction was added to the mentioned editions for the benefit of those Italian readers who, having a basic knowledge of Spanish, wanted to read the literary works in their original language. It can also be suggested that Delicado's explicit interest in providing the Italian audience with guidelines to read and understand Spanish reflects the suspicion that these editions, rather than having been prepared principally for the Spaniards in Italy, were largely directed to an Italian audience.[13] It is worth noting that Delicado's interest in his Italian readers parallels that of Juan de Valdés, who, in 1535, was writing the *Diálogo de la lengua* (Dialogue of the Language) for his Neapolitan friends.[14] In sixteenth-century Italy it was fashionable to know Spanish, and Delicado made a meritorious effort to facilitate the process of learning the new language. His didactic treatise on Spanish and Italian phonetics had a long repercussion in Italy,[15] as did his editions of *Celestina* and of the chivalric romances which have continued to enjoy considerable fame.[16]

CHAPTER 2

General Considerations on Portrait of Lozana: *The Exuberant Andalusian Woman*

I *The Plot of* Lozana

LOZANA is born in Cordova, the offspring of a gambler-pimp and a clothier. Her birthname is Aldonza, but she is soon given the name of Lozana to complement her beauty and exuberance.[1] When she is in her teens, her father dies, leaving the mother involved in legal disputes. After the conclusion of the litigation, Lozana and her mother move to Jerez, where the mother dies. Deprived of both parents, she goes to Seville to reside with an aunt, who soon introduces her to a wealthy merchant, Diomedes, whose mistress she becomes. She travels with him to several Mediterranean cities until Diomedes's father requests him to return home to Marseilles to report on his business ventures. Diomedes complies, and he takes along Lozana, who now has children by him. In the meantime the father has learned with displeasure about his son's connection with Lozana. When the two appear in Marseilles, the father puts his son into prison and orders a boatman to take Lozana out to sea to be drowned. The boatman, however, is more tenderhearted than the father; he gives her one of his garments and allows her to land at Leghorn. With the money she receives from the sale of a ring she had hidden in her mouth, Lozana travels to Rome.

In the Eternal City Lozana finds a group of Spanish women who give her lodging. After staying with them briefly, she quarrels with them and then moves on to a part of the city called Pozo Blanco. One day while walking through the streets of Pozo Blanco, Lozana is seen by a Sevillian woman, a shirtmaker, who invites her into her house. Soon they are joined by other women, and Lozana gives them an account of her origins and life. The women are impressed with Lozana's loquacity and exuberance. She reveals her *converso* background, a fact which endears her even more to the women who are also New Christians. Subsequently, Lozana inquires about the presence and life of the Jews in Rome. She expresses a desire to learn more of the Jewish technique for preparing cosmetics, and she is directed to a Neapolitan woman, a shopkeeper in the district of Calabraga. After meeting the Neapolitan woman and revealing her wisdom in the beautifying arts, Lozana begs that the woman's son, Rampín, be allowed to show her the city. Lozana marvels at its wonders and is delighted with her guide, whom she invites to sleep with her the first night.

The following day Rampín accompanies Lozana to the Jewish district of Rome. There she is introduced to a shrewd businessman named Trigo, who, seeing the potentials of the attractive Andalusian woman, provides her with a house. Lozana now establishes herself as a courtesan, with Rampín as her servant and pimp. In this profession she excels, being constantly motivated by a natural propensity to deceive and to improve her economic well-being. Her first clients are a chief waiter, a mace bearer and a mail carrier, all of whom she defrauds. Lozana's wit and astuteness become apparent. Following the episode of the three clients, the Andalusian woman is sent by Trigo to visit a courtesan who is suffering from a maternity ailment. Lozana recommends the remedy. She also treats an illness of the prelate responsible for the courtesan's pregnancy, only to become herself pregnant by him.

At the beginning of part 2, Lozana meets an ambassador's servant and the author, who appears in the novel as a character. Asked for advice on how to succeed in their amorous goals, Lozana tells one to pay money and the other to eat sage. Subsequently, Lozana herself tricks a gentleman's attendant into giving her money for a cape as the price of love. Lozana's activities as a trickster continue first at the house of a wealthy man, from whom she obtains coal to heat her house, and later in a sex game she plays with two suitors. Following a dream which Lozana has of Rampín falling into the river, the young boy is caught stealing fruit and is taken to prison. Freed from prison, he falls into a latrine. He is rescued by Lozana and a friend. In search of better fortune, Lozana decides to look for a new residence. She meets a squire who prognosticates future social chaos. This does not worry the Andalusian woman, who continues to give practical advice to courtesans and aspiring courtesans. While searching for a new house, Lozana meets an ambassador and a gentleman. The gentleman asks Lozana to serve as a go-between for the ambassador. Lozana consents, but first, with the pretext of being poor, she solicits money for the rent of her house. She uses a similar technique to deceive other admirers and to secure money from them.

Part 3 begins with a long soliloquy by Lozana. Tired of being involved with courtesans, Lozana decides to become more autonomous. The author-character reappears. He admonishes the Andalusian woman for taking advantage of people's ignorance and superstitious beliefs. Later he concurs with Lozana's argument that to be able to survive one must resort to everything, including deception. Lozana contemplates nostalgically the rapidly deteriorating life of the courtesans. She proposes that a place of shelter and refuge be provided for the old courtesans to ensure greater opportunities for younger ones. Recognizing the unfavorable conditions of the courtesans, the Andalusian woman begins to rely less on her abilities as a courtesan and more on her beautifying skills. She is visited continuously by women in need of help. Shortly after having reverted to her old profession, Lozana herself becomes the object of a trick by two ruffians who manage to seduce her without pay. At the end of her vicissitudes the Andalusian woman advises a young lover on how to regain his sweetheart who has married an old man against her will. Lozana also makes a final round of the city selling cosmetics, for which she obtains a considerable amount of money. Tired of her earthly activities and disillusioned with the world around her, Lozana resolves to leave Rome and move to the island of Lipari in hope of finding peace.

II *The Structure of* Lozana

Although the structure of *Lozana* will be examined in detail in chapter 6, a brief discussion of it is presented here to facilitate reference.

The novel is composed of two main parts: the author's narration and the protagonists' dialogue, with an additional and very brief epistle delivered by Lozana to the women of Rome. The bulk of the work is written in dialogue form. The structural components of *Lozana* are: Dedication, Plot description, Part I, Part II, Apology of the author, Explanation of content, Epilogue, author's Letter of excommunication against a woman of ill repute, Lozana's Epistle, author's Digression.

Part I and Part II are divided into sixty-six *mamotretos* ("memoranda"). The division of *Lozana* into "memoranda," instead of the traditional division into chapters, enhances the author's ostensible intention of giving a faithful account of the events in Rome. The result is a diary-type novel. Central to the work is the representation of Lozana's life as a courtesan and go-between, and her roguish adventures with Rampín in the Eternal City; for this reason it has an affinity to the celestinesque novel and to the picaresque genre.

In the dialogue portion of the novel as well as before and after it, there are moralizations and didactic considerations presented by Delicado, as author and as character, and by some of the other personages. These moral reflections have a direct relationship to Lozana's licentious conduct and to the social corruption of the time. Contributing to the work's moral thoughts are the fruits of personal experience, as well as the adages of classical antiquity, of the Bible, and of folkloric tradition. There are more than 150 proverbs in *Lozana,* many of which complement the moral-didactic purpose of the work, which is to show the futility of, and disillusionment with, human endeavors.

III *The History of* Lozana *Criticism*

The *Portrait of Lozana: The Exuberant Andalusian Woman* was written in Rome between 1513 and 1527 and it was revised and published anonymously in Venice in 1528. The work remained in obscurity until the mid-nineteenth century when the German philologist Ferdinand Wolf discovered the only existing copy of the Venetian edition at the Imperial Library of Vienna. Wolf made the discovery public in an article and in his *History of Spanish and Portuguese Literature.*[2] His works, however, must not have been known to many Spanish, French, and Italian critics who attributed, instead, the discovery of the work to the Spanish bibliophile Pascual de Gayangos, who was the first to identify the author.[3] Shortly thereafter, in 1857, Gayangos also made two transcriptions of the work. These transcriptions, very poor copies of the original, served as the basis of scholarship for many years to come.

Nineteenth-century criticism of *Lozana* was fundamentally unfavorable although, at times, ambivalent. The puritanical scholars of the time were scandalized at some of the work's more risqué scenes. They praised the novel, however, for its lively language, rich popular jargon, and for its vivid representation of social customs and manners.[4] In fact, Luis de Lara, who prepared an edition of *Lozana,* advised his readers to "close an eye" on the presumed "obscenity" of the work and to look instead at the novel's exquisite language. Concerning *Lozana's* literary affiliation, some critics considered the work akin to Pietro Aretino's *Ragionamenti* (Discussions), suggesting a possible influence of Aretino on Delicado. The French scholar Alcide Bonneau noted, however, that for chronological reasons such influences would have been impossible; quite to the contrary, Bonneau asserted, if there were an influence it would have originated with Delicado.[5]

Twentieth-century criticism of *Lozana* began with the expression of that same attraction toward, and repulsion from, the work, that had characterized the criticism of the earlier period.[6] *Lozana* began to be acknowledged as an important historical document of Renaissance Rome and as a valuable book of sixteenth-century folklore, but its "eccentricity" continued to shock the moral sense of the critics. Menéndez Pelayo, for example,[7] referred to *Lozana* as a work consisting of a "parade of sinners and of pornographic scenes."[8] From the point of *Lozana's* literary affiliation, some early twentieth-century scholars began to see perceptively an affinity not only with Aretino's works[9] but also with Juan Ruiz's *Libro de buen amor* (Book of Good Love) and Alfonso Martínez de Toledo's *Corbacho o reprobación del amor mundano* ("Whip" or Reprobation of Mundane Love).[10]

In 1942 José Gómez de la Serna gave new direction to *Lozana* criticism by asserting that Delicado's novel is fundamentally a moral work. In the introduction to his edition of *Lozana*, the critic expressed the view that the Inquisition had been responsible for concealing the work, originally, by placing it on the index of forbidden books. This, Gómez de la Serna contended, was done because of the "poor mentality" of the Inquisitorial authorities who failed to see the moral didactic message of *Lozana*. "If they had analyzed the work with a serene and just mind," asserted Gómez de la Serna, "they would have seen that the moral background of the work lies precisely in the unglorified picture of the courtesans and in the representation of the physical and moral dangers which accompany those who associate with them. . . ."[11] Gómez de la Serna studied *Lozana* also from an artistic and literary perspective. He stressed the importance of the plastic quality of the work's dialogue and the spontaneity and naturalness of its language. He further related *Lozana* to the picaresque genre, particularly to *Lazarillo* and *Guzmán de Alfarache*,[12] thus placing the work in the mainstream of humanistic literature.

In 1950 there was published a facsimile edition of *Lozana*, which finally gave the world an exact copy of Delicado's work.[13] Following the appearance of the facsimile, interest in *Lozana* grew significantly, as can be seen from the three doctoral dissertations and the more than twenty scholarly articles that have been written on it. Increased interest in Delicado's novel has also been manifested by the publication of eight editions[14] of *Lozana*. In 1952 Antonio Vilanova prepared the first edition of *Lozana* based on the facsimile copy.[15] Although the text of his edition contains numerous errors, Vilanova's introduction provided the best and most thorough commentary that had ever been written on Delicado and his novel. Vilanova not only advanced some interesting theories about the author's Jewish background, he also studied *Lozana* from its proper historical and artistic perspective. He presented an inspiring analysis of the novel's topographic and social setting. Furthermore, he considered *Lozana* an important work of transition between *Celestina* and the picaresque novel, because of its realism, satire, and materialistic philosophy.[16] In addition, Vilanova offered some original ideas on Delicado's relationship to Cervantes, from the point of view of characterization and of the author's personal appearance in his work.[17]

Bruce Wardropper followed Vilanova in opening the way to the modern studies on *Lozana*. Professor Wardropper made a penetrating examination of Delicado's concept of his novel as a literary portrait. He looked upon *Lozana* as a work of art which was unjustly neglected because of the exaggerated puritanical criticism of Menéndez Pelayo. Wardropper rightly dismissed the early twentieth-century misguided judgment on Delicado's novel while stressing the artistic merit of *Lozana* based on the colorful, ingenious, and realistic representation of a woman and of the world around her.[18] More recently, such merits of Delicado and his novel have also been discussed by Segundo Serrano Poncela, who asserts that *Lozana* "demands a place of greater recognition in Spanish literature."[19] Serrano Poncela relates *Lozana* to the Renaissance "joie de vivre," and its satirical and moral tone to the Erasmian currents of the time. He also discusses Delicado's originality in relation to the realistic portrayal of the protagonist.

Other scholars such as Thomas Mocas,[20] Lester Beberfall,[21] and Manuel Criado de Val[22] have laboriously studied the linguistic aspects of *Lozana*, its lexicography in general, and its Italianisms and erotic language in particular. Their studies reveal the importance of *Lozana*'s linguistic wealth, which comes both from literary tradition as well as from the real world whose sounds Delicado attempted to reproduce in his portrait of Renaissance Rome. Interest in

Delicado's novel has also been manifested by Albert Ian Bagby, who has found some stimulating parallels between Lozana, the exuberant Andalusian woman, and Don Juan in the drama of Tirso de Molina. Such similarities would consist of ingenuity, sagacity, astuteness, savoir faire, and a spirit of conquest. Because of these characteristics and the fact that Lozana is, with few exceptions, the initiator and the aggressor in her relations with men, Bagby refers to her as a "doña Juana."[23]

The development of *Lozana* criticism has reached a significant stage with the very perceptive study of José Antonio Hernández on the artistic originality of Delicado's novel. This fine scholar has elaborated on certain basic aspects of *Lozana*'s entertaining and didactic purpose and on its historical significance. He has also provided a keen analysis of the main protagonist, considering such aspects as Lozana's wit, ingenuity, and sense of freedom. Hernández shows that Lozana is, in fact, an extremely well-delineated character, an exceptional figure which combines the realism of daily existence with a spirit of idealism. In addition to discussing these and other interesting points of *Lozana,* Hernández has expounded on the very important relationship between Erasmus's *Praise of Folly* and Delicado's novel, a relationship which underlines *Lozana*'s moral didactic purpose.[24]

IV Conclusion

In summary, the following observations point up the evolution of *Lozana* criticism: (1) Delicado's novel which in the nineteenth and early twentieth centuries was an inexplainable and censured work has, in recent years, been understood and acclaimed as a great work of art; (2) the traditional view of *Lozana* as a novel having little or no relationship to literary tradition has been replaced by consideration of Delicado's work as a creation of notable literary affinity; (3) in general terms, the historical significance of *Lozana* had always been recognized, although modern critics have identified with greater precision the historical components of the novel; the same is true of *Lozana*'s idiomatic and linguistic importance; (4) modern interpretations of realism have led scholars to a greater understanding and appreciation of Delicado's concept of literary portraiture.

CHAPTER 3

Influences on Lozana

BECAUSE of *Lozana*'s singular faithfulness to the historical circumstance of Renaissance Rome it has been said that the work "was born of life and not of books."[1] Although, as we shall see, there is much to be said for *Lozana*'s affinity with the sociohistorical condition of its times, it is well to remember that Delicado is not only a chronicler but also an artist of considerable literary sensibility. His art is nourished by his knowledge of literary tradition, and it is the purpose of this chapter to discuss Delicado's awareness of this tradition as it is manifested in *Lozana* and to show the possible influences on his work.

I *Classical Influences*

It is not surprising that Delicado should seek the model of his work in the life of men and women of his times, in the world around him. Already, at the beginning of the sixteenth century, a notable interest was manifested in the Aristotelian precepts which demand, of the poet no less than of the artist, the imitation of nature.[2] "Just as the Greeks achieved eminence by taking Nature . . . as their preceptor, so modern Spaniards, it was said, could — indeed must — do the same."[3]

Aristotle is the most important source of inspiration for Delicado's efforts to represent the world of Renaissance Rome in a truthful manner. Delicado's knowledge of Aristotle's *Poetics* and of his concept of verisimilitude is reflected everywhere in *Lozana,* where the Aristotelian dictum "Truth is a better friend" is cited (Digression, 259)[4] and put to practice. Following Aristotelian precepts, Delicado manifests a veracious attitude, insists on representing men as they are, and compares, symbolically, his task as a writer to that of the painters (Plot, 35-36), who in the Renaissance sought their model in nature.

Delicado's objective, to base his artistic creation on the reality of the world around him and to depict that reality with a didactic purpose, can be related to Aristotle's teleological thought. The philosopher teaches that life is to be understood not in terms of its elements alone but in terms of its ends. Aristotle's interpretation of life stems from his close observation of the norms, standards, and ideals of Greek culture and civilization, and from his belief that man's lack of wisdom leads him to pursue a bad or inadequate end, such as pleasure or money.[5] Delicado learns from the philosopher not only a deep concern with the reality that surrounds him but he also assimilates thoughts on practical intelligence, theoretical wisdom, and moral virtue.

In the Dedication of *Lozana* Delicado shows that he was also inspired by another classical writer, Juvenal. The Spanish writer underlines the integrity of his literary portrait by affirming that its constituent parts are drawn only from things which he himself heard and saw, as did Juvenal in reporting the events of his times (Dedication, 33). In fact, Juvenal, the historical chronicler, served as an author-witness model for Delicado, and his famed satirical sketches of ancient Rome, mentioned in *Lozana* as an example that is being imitated, reinforces the sincerity of Delicado's portrait.[6] In addition to Juvenal, another Roman writer, Persius, served as a model to Delicado. Persius, a remarkable satirist who sternly censured the immorality and superstitions of his day, is recalled in *Lozana* in connection with the protagonist's beliefs in omens and the supernatural (XLII, 174).[7] What is important to the author of *Lozana* is that everything about his subject be totally and candidly disclosed, and he relates the frankness of his work to the idea of yet another classical figure, Cicero, who asserted that "a letter does not blush" (Dedication, 34).[8] If Cicero inspired Delicado to produce an audaciously truthful portrait of Rome, Seneca taught him that "a little eloquence is enough to tell the truth" (Plot, 35),[9] a lesson with which he defends the unpretentious style of his work.

Delicado's immediate model is Roman society, in general, and a woman, Lozana, in particular. His portrait of this woman is so "natural" that "there is no one who, having ever met Lozana, . . . would say that it is not drawn from her actions, manners, and words" (Plot, 35 - 36). In portraying Lozana as a woman of creative character and astuteness, the author considers her as a follower of Seneca, seen as a model of conduct (XLIX, 194). To give an idea of her eloquence Delicado compares her to Demosthenes, the greatest orator of ancient Greece (Plot, 36),[10] and to characterize the glorious national background of Lozana, he cites the celebrated poets Lucan and Martial as her distinguished ancestors.

Classical antiquity provided Delicado with a philosophy and a model for his "truthful representation" of Roman life, sources of inspiration for the delineation of his major protagonist and, also, an example of the didactic purpose possible in a work of art. For this it is very likely that Delicado relied on Apuleius's *Metamorphoses,* commonly known as *The Golden Ass*. Apuleius's work had been translated into Castilian toward the end of the fifteenth century by Diego López de Cortegana, who published his translation in Seville around 1513. With subsequent translations of *The Golden Ass* the work grew in popularity and influence and became one of the best-liked classical works in Spain.[11]

The reader will recall that *The Golden Ass* is a conglomeration of short stories, told in autobiographical form, inserted into the framework of the tale of a youth (Lucius Apuleius) whose misdirected curiosity changed him into an ass while retaining human perceptions. These short and amusing stories, presented with much realism, range from the ribald to the romantic, from tales of robbers to those of religious racketeers, but in all of them the author appears as a keen and satirical observer of the contemporary scene which he depicts in its almost limitless variety. To the autobiographical form, the realism of presentation and the satirical intention, Apuleius adds another important element in his story: a religious meaning. For this, Apuleius presents, first, the tale of Cupid and Psyche which can be interpreted as an element of Platonic allegory: the salvation of the Human Soul (Psyche) by Love (Cupid). Second, Apuleius depicts the protagonist Lucius as a devout believer in the goddess Isis, a devotion which will regain for him his natural human condition, which he lost when the misuse of magical powers turned him into an animal. And, once Lucius repents, and consequently regains his proper form, he retires from all worldly activity, thus providing an ending common to later picaresque novels.

Delicado's familiarity with Apuleius's work can be seen, first, in Lozana's comparison of her life with that of the protagonist Lucius Apuleius: " . . . I wanted to know and see and experience like Apuleius, and at the end I found that all was vanity . . ." (LIV, 207). Second, Delicado manifests his knowledge of *The Golden Ass* in the ironic comparison which another character in *Lozana,* Porfirio, makes between his donkey Robusto and the transformed Lucius Apuleius (LXV, 242). Delicado's acquaintance with the classical work can further be observed in the way in which the Spanish writer concludes the last memorandum of his novel by imploring God to help him flee human temptation and vanity (LXVI, 246). This is consistent with the ideological intention of conveying a moral lesson through the realization of the futility of human delights as seen particularly in the last book of *The Golden Ass* where the transformed hero of the work is regenerated through the Mysteries of Isis. It should be noted that for Cortegana, the Spanish translator of *The Golden Ass*, the didactic intention of the work was of extreme significance, as he demonstrates in the introduction to his translation. Delicado not only knew of Cortegana's moral interpretation of *The Golden Ass* but he also adapted many of the ideas and concepts expressed in Cortegana's prefatory remarks.[12]

Less significant but worth noting nevertheless is Delicado's knowledge of another classical writer, the gastronomer Marcus Apitius, to whom is falsely attributed a work entitled *De re coquinaria* (On Culinary Art). The exhaustive list of culinary preparations in this work and in a play of the sixteenth century, the *Comedia Serafina*, probably inspired Delicado to include in *Lozana* some very descriptive pages of gastronomic delicacies. The enumeration of culinary specialities in memorandum II gives evidence of Lozana's profoundly Andalusian background, and it provides us with an interesting aspect of the popular traditions and customs of the time.

II Biblical Influences

The development of Western European literature has been profoundly influenced by one of man's greatest literary masterpieces, the Bible. The spiritual and intellectual teachings of Holy Scripture became an integral part of medieval thought and letters, and they continued to occupy a prominent position in the mind and literature of the Spanish Renaissance. This can be seen, to some extent, in Delicado's works.

The author's knowledge of Sacred Scripture is reflected best in the treatise *On the Use of the West Indies' Wood*, although it is also apparent in *Lozana*. In memorandum XXIII, the majordomo remarks to a courtesan that "when the head hurts all the members are affected" (p. 109). His words are a probable Biblical reference to a passage in a letter of Saint Paul to the Corinthians: "If one member suffers, all suffer together" (1 Cor. 12:26). This passage, which is part of Saint Paul's epistle on the relation of the head to the members of the Mystical Body of Christ, could have a symbolic meaning in

Lozana where Rome, the seat of Christianity, is seen also as the center of corruption which affects everyone. Such moral interpretation is strengthened by another reference which the author makes to Saint Paul, in memorandum XLII. There Lozana discusses her celestinesque talents, her life and Roman activities with the author-protagonist who, upon seeing that wine is brought to him, comments on the beverage as a source of lust. His words *in quo est luxuria* ("in which there is lust") reminds us of the advice which Paul gives to the Ephesians *Nolite inebriari vino in quo est luxuria* ("Do not get drunk with wine, for that is debauchery") (Eph. 5:18). Lozana herself is well aware of the dangerous effects of wine as she cites the popular saying, "Who made you a whore? Wine and fruit" (XII, 63), traditionally viewed as the cause and symbol of sin. Delicado, the moralist, sees Lozana and, by extension, Rome, as the embodiment of sin: "All of you [courtesans] have a propensity to evil and envy," Delicado tells the Andalusian woman (XLII, 177). Because of this, he tries to mend her ways, and the habits of Rome, by stressing the importance of believing in God: " . . . you must believe in your Creator, who is omnipotent and is the source of strength and virtue . . ." (XLII, 177).

The author, living in a world where human folly prevails, recognizes the strong efforts that must be made to avoid the occasion of sin in order that he may be saved, and thus he seeks inspiration in another biblical source, the psalmist's words: "Turn away my eyes, Lord, that they may not see vanity" (Ps. 118:37). But Delicado himself succumbs to his human weakness and he does see vanity, as a result of which he experiences spiritual torment and severe corporal suffering. For this he blames a woman on whom he casts the biblical damnation that befell the cities of Sodom and Gomorrah (Gen. 18 - 19), and on Dathan and Abiram who conspired against Moses (Letter of excommunication, 256; Ps. 106:17).

From Holy Scripture Delicado draws also the example of the talking ass. The folktale of Balaam's ass in the Bible (Num. 22: 23 - 28), which reflects oriental humor, undoubtedly inspired Delicado's jocose episode in which Robusto, the ass, learns to read (LXV, 241).[13]

III   *Medieval Influences*

If *Lozana* demonstrates the influence of some classical and biblical writings, it also shows traces of the style and philosophy of certain Spanish medieval works. Among these is the *Libro de Buen Amor*

(Book of Good Love) by Juan Ruiz, Archpriest of Hita. With this work *Lozana* shares a profoundly comic and satirical attitude, a didactic intention combined with artistic virtuosity and a common philosophy of life. The *Book of Good Love* is the story of a good-humored, jovial cleric in search of amorous adventures. The protagonist affirms that he should strive for *buen amor* ("spiritual love") but he gives, instead, a vivid picture of *loco amor* ("worldly love"), with much keen satire. Juan Ruiz declares that his intention in writing the *Book of Good Love* is "to gladden the body and benefit the soul."[14] To delight the reader, Ruiz resorts to a number of poetic devices common in the tradition of medieval laughter:[15] humorous scenes, onomatopoeic puns, verses extolling sensual pleasures, parodies of aristocratic and courtly literature and of religious themes. Ruiz, however, reminds us that beneath this poetic virtuosity there is to be found a deeper meaning: "The jest you hear, do not believe that it is idle chaff / The book has subtle meaning beneath each joyous laugh."[16]

As we shall see in chapter 6, Delicado also cloaks the moral lesson beneath skillfully contrived artistic means. His genial representation of man's pursuit of pleasure possesses an undeniable jollity and humor reminiscent of the *Book of Good Love* and of the tradition of medieval jocose literature, which is, stylistically, an antithesis of the "tragic" and aristocratic literature of love and chivalry.[17] As will be shown, the seemingly risqué passages of *Lozana* are designed to evoke laughter, not passion. Following the model of distinguished predecessors, Delicado, like Juan Ruiz, recognizes that "between one laugh and another it is well to speak the truth."[18] The truth in both *Lozana* and the *Book of Good Love* is that, in the psalmist's words, "men's thoughts are vanity" (Ps. 94:11).

Lozana also reflects the influence of the *Book of Good Love* in the value of humor as a means of satirizing the clergy. Among the best-known passages of anticlerical satire in the *Book of Good Love* is the one on the "Canonical hours." This passage, burlesque and parodic in nature, as Corominas asserts,[19] is aimed at the licentious conduct of clerics behaving like "members of a band of thieves" who eagerly seize the opportunity of seducing women.[20] Also reflected in the pages of *Lozana* is the widely known discourse on the power of money "which makes lies true and truth lies," with respect to greedy clerics.[21]

In his satirical treatment of clerical vanity and corruption Delicado does not fail to take up this theme of money and clerics as found in the *Book of Good Love* and in the goliardic poetry of the Middle Ages, and to reiterate the intimate relationship which exists between the man of the cloth and money. The personified Love in Ruiz's work reminds the protagonist of the necessity to be generous with his procuress, to assure her aid, as well as with the woman to be conquered. In Delicado's book Lozana herself is a frequent beneficiary of such clerical generosity as are a number of other courtesans. This can be seen, for example, in the passage in which Lozana directs the servant Jacomina not to awaken the mistress of the house "since the abbot did not let her sleep all night": "He must have already gone to the chancery for money" affirms Lozana, who adds: "there he will extort contributions from some poor man so as to continue to be in the good graces of your mistress" (XXXV, 149 - 150). The view of enamored and mundane clerics is meaningful in both the *Book of Good Love* and in *Lozana*. The attacks against them are carried forth by caricature, irony, and satire, and it is significant that Juan Ruiz and Delicado — both clerics — present themselves in their works as sinners, as examples of the very mundaneness which they censure, a fact which reinforces their didactic intention.[22]

Lozana is thus akin to Juan Ruiz's book in the stimulating and intriguing portrayal of worldly love, in the ostensibly didactic intention, and in the artistic way to fulfill it, and, lastly, in the philosophy of life which it presents. Juan Ruiz declares: "As Aristotle said and said truly: The world lives for two things. The first is to have food and lodging and the other to procure union with a pleasing woman."[23] Men, like the animals, asserts the Archpriest, desire by their nature a constant succession of new mates and every man thinks continually of how he can accomplish this. Such amatory philosophy dominates also the pages of *Lozana* where the prime mover is love and the pursuit of pleasure exemplified by the protagonist, to whom everyone succumbs and from whom everyone derives hope (XXIV, 114).

In addition to displaying certain artistic and ideological similarities with the *Book of Good Love,* Delicado's novel also manifests an affinity to other works of the late Middle Ages, which possibly served as literary models to *Lozana*. Quite apparent are, for example, various novelistic parallels between *Lozana* and the *Corbacho* ("Whip") written in 1438 by Alonso Martínez de Toledo, Archpriest of Talavera. In essence, this work is a bitter satire against the vices of woman: flirt, adulteress, gossip, conceited beauty. The author, well acquainted with this subject, gives a good insight into the private and everyday life of women of his day and provides us with sketches of contemporary society drawn with a vivacity and brilliance that are truly remarkable.

The points of contact between *Lozana* and *Corbacho* rest on their fundamentally similar vision of women and, more importantly, on their artistic composition which approaches that of a literary painting. With regard to the first of these points, it is very possible that Delicado saw in *Corbacho* a literary model for the antifeminist spirit which he projects in *Lozana* where women's material ambitions and lust lead men to their downfall. Lozana and other courtesans in Delicado's work become that symbol of pride, greed, and deception which typifies women of *Corbacho*.[24] Lozana, for example, feigns being a respectable married woman, confesses to being a thief and, to improve her fortune, she becomes a fraudulent practitioner of the healing arts, thus deceiving and stealing at will. And to complement her contention of being the best and most talented courtesan in Rome she resorts to a variety of seductive techniques.

To be sure, Delicado does not manifest toward his female protagonist the severe attitude that Martínez de Toledo shows for women, but he appears, nevertheless, scornful of their activities and concerned about the physical and spiritual dangers which they bring on themselves and on others. In a vein which recalls the moralistic sentiments of the Archpriest of Talavera, Delicado tells us, in the concluding pages of his work, that women "think and act in ways that they would not if they had the beginning of wisdom, which is the fear of God" (Apology, 248).

Lozana also shows an influence of the *Corbacho* in its style and, particularly, in the author's point of view. Characterized as a "talkative and entertaining painter of national habits,"[25] the Archpriest of Talavera undoubtedly offered Delicado another artistic model for his affirmation of having witnessed the events described in *Lozana*. The following statements which the Archpriest of Talavera makes with respect to his literary technique represent a definite precedent to Delicado's own art. Martínez de Toledo declares the purpose of his treatise: "Seeing such evil and harm, I proposed to write and talk to some extent about this material,"[26] and later, upon talking about a cause of this evil, that is, a woman known to him: "I saw her the other day; that one whom you regard as beautiful and whom you praise so. . . ."[27] And toward the end of his work: "But I want to tell you only a little bit of another licentious friar, whom I saw with my own eyes. . . ."[28] What accompanies each of these statements is a narrative characterized by keen observation and vital language that Delicado will later incorporate into his literary portrait. In some instances the Archpriest of Talavera displays a good ability for dialogue whose potential "theatrical quality"[29] attains a real dramatic character in *Lozana.*

Delicado's insistence in representing only what he sees and hears reminds us also of the *Generaciones y semblanzas* (Generations and Sketches) by Fernán Pérez de Guzmán, who is praised by the Swiss historian Fueter, for his "psychological perspicacity, precise knowledge of the world, independent judgment and realism in expression."[30] The *Generations and Sketches,* written about 1440, form a series of portraits with emphasis on "the characteristics and national habits," and on the "lineages and features and conditions"[31] of the principal men of his age. The important thing for this fifteenth-century historian, as for Delicado later, is to create a literary portrait based upon evident elements. Consequently, the first principle of the historian is "that he be present to the principal and notable acts of war and peace,"[32] a rule which Delicado follows vigorously.

For his literary and historical portrait Delicado was also inspired by the work of another writer of the late Middle Ages, Hernando del Pulgar, whom he cites in the preliminary pages of *Lozana.* Pulgar, a royal counselor, emissary, and chronicler, is famous for a number of historical writings, but he is particularly well-known for his *Claros varones de Castilla* (Illustrious Men of Castile, 1486), a collection of biographies of great figures of Enrique IV's court. In the dedicatory pages of his work, Pulgar emphasizes the thoroughness of his undertaking by suggesting that he will offer a detailed account of the lineage, profession, and deeds of those celebrated men of Castile.[33] Pulgar's systematic technique in narrating the life of his compatriots served as a model to Delicado, who also insists that the first thing that must be told in his portrait is Lozana's birthplace and parentage, her fortune, misfortune, and success, her manners and loquaciousness (Plot, 35).

Delicado not only saw Pulgar's *Generations* as a model for the methodical presentation of Lozana's life, but he also perceived and was enlightened by the intense expressiveness, profound humanity, and charm of his predecessor's biographical portraits. Professor Domínguez Bordona considers Pulgar's artistry in terms of his ability to capture, in a completely modern fashion, the totality of his personages' traits: their passions, virtues, weaknesses, and vices,[34] a talent, we can add, that is also a part of Delicado's literary skills.

In addition to the above-mentioned authors and works, Delicado was also familiar with the works of the fifteenth-century poet Antón de Montoro, a Jewish convert from Cordova, whose satiric and burlesque wit he sometimes imitates, and to whom Lozana is compared for her clever and ironic speech. Furthermore, the author of *Lozana* displays an acquaintance with such medieval ballads as the *Romancero del Cid* (Ballads of the Cid) and the *Romance de Abenámar* (Ballad of Abenámar). From these Delicado takes the names of the Count of Carrión (envious and shameful count in the poem of the *Cid*)[35] and Abenámar (a celebrated Moorish prince),[36] and applies them burlesquely to Rampín (XXXIII, 144; XXXIV, 148).

Another medieval work with which Delicado was familiar, and which served as the source of a passage in *Lozana,* is the famous collection of comical sketches written by Pietro Gonnella, the jester at the Court of Ferrara, in the early part of the fourteenth century. He has been characterized as a swindler, as a man without scruples who is moved by his desire for profit and is always jocular. Gonnella became a legendary figure and his fame was subsequently augmented by such writers as Franco Sacchetti in *Trecentonovelle* (Three Hundred Short Stories, 1390) and by Poggio Bracciolini in his *Facetiae* (Humorous Pleasantries, 1415). The facts and legends of Gonnella's life and buffooneries reached their highest diffusion in the beginning of the sixteenth century.[37] That is when Delicado became acquainted with the stories of Gonnella, one of which he reports in memorandum LIV of *Lozana*.

IV Folkloric Influences

It has long been recognized that *Lozana* is a valuable document of Spanish folklore. In fact, the work derives much of its uniqueness from the representation of traditions, beliefs and customs, gathered from a variety of sources. Popular writings and the oral tradition, in particular, influenced significantly Delicado's style as is evidenced by the more than 150 proverbial expressions that are used in *Lozana.* Similarly, the popular tradition makes itself felt in *Lozana,* in the mention of such legendary figures as Lazarillo (XXXV, 151);[38] Bartolomé del Puerto (XXXIV, 119),[39] a type of Don Juan; Pedro de Urdemalas (LI, 198),[40] the joker; Hernán Centeno (LI, 198), a celebrated impostor; Pedro Aguilocho (XXXVII, 157),[41] the thief; Merlín, the legendary enchanter (LXIII, 238); and Juan Desperaendios (LXII, 236),[42] the Wandering Jew. The richness of the popular tradition in *Lozana* can also be seen in the reference to various other folkloric figures as the "newly married man from Hornachuelos" (XXXVII, 157),[43] the unwanted suitor, the "Jewish woman of Zaragoza" (IX, 56)[44] who enjoyed meddling in other people's business, and Maricastaña (XXXVII, 159), the proverbial woman who became a symbol of remote times. Worth mentioning also, as part of the folkloric influences on Delicado's work, is the *Song of Gómez Arias*,[45] a verse of which, "nunca en tal me vi" ("I have never seen myself in such a situation"), is repeated by Lozana.

V Renaissance Influences

One of the most important literary sources of *Lozana* is the *Tragicomedia de Calisto y Melibea* (Tragicomedy of Calixtus and Melibea), more popularly known as *Celestina,* first published in Burgos, in 1499. It reached wide diffusion in Italy, particularly after the Roman edition of 1506. The fact that Delicado looked on *Celestina* as a model is reflected in the title page of *Lozana* where we read that "it contains many more things than the *Celestina."* Furthermore, in the Dedication of *Lozana* the author makes a playful allusion to the major character of *Celestina,* ". . . that woman who lived in Salamanca in the epoch of Celestine II . . ." (Dedication, 33).[46] Delicado knew and admired *Celestina* as is evidenced by these and other references to the work (XXXVII, 155; LII, 200). Furthermore, Lozana, who apparently was in the habit of having some literary compositions read to her, asks her friends to read *Celestina,* which she greatly enjoyed (XLVII, 190).

There are a number of interesting parallels between *Lozana* and *Celestina,* which suggest that the latter had a notable influence upon Delicado's work. From every textual indication, the beautiful, sensual, and astute protagonist in Delicado's novel is a perfect copy of the way Celestina herself must have been in her youthful years. Lozana, like her predecessor, acquires wisdom through the experience of life which teaches her to be audacious and perceptive and also to be contemptuous of loneliness and poverty. Like Celestina, Delicado's protagonist also plays the role of *alcahueta* (procuress) for distressed lovers, although, within the context of sixteenth-century Rome, the "go-between" loses much of her original importance.

In *Lozana,* as in *Celestina,* physical love is the primary moving force. The pursuit of love and pleasures in both works reflects the glorification of life and the enjoyment of the moment which was so prevalent in Renaissance culture. Delicado's knowledge of Bartolomé dei Sacchi's *De voluptatibus* (On Pleasures, II, 39), gives evidence of his insight into the literary as well as the real concern which the society of the time had for enjoymènt. The author of *Celestina* made an artistic representation of that Renaissance world of pleasure and delight but he interjected, also, a moral thesis through philosophical observations and the ultimate death of the foolish lovers, Calisto and Melibea. Delicado introduces a similar ideological intention through various moralizing statements and the sack of Rome, seen as a providential punishment.

The influence of *Celestina* on Delicado's work is observed also in the structure and language of *Lozana*. Following the example of the model, *Lozana* is divided in dialogistic scenes in which a lively, "spoken language"[47] enhances the dimension of realism. The conversation, frequently elliptical and witty, and abounding with proverbs in *Celestina*, undoubtedly inspired Delicado to treat with the same vigor and colloquial charm the conversations of his characters. It is possible that Delicado also found inspiration for his work in another literary creation of the time: the *Cuestión de amor* (Question of Love), a sentimental novel published anonymously in Naples, in 1510. This novel is a social document of manners which depicts with great fidelity aristocratic life in Naples during the early sixteenth century. The historical value of the work has been recognized by various critics, including Benedetto Croce, who has deciphered the identity of a number of veiled personages.[48]

The author of the *Question of Love* is still unknown, although his identity has been studied in relation to one of his characters, Felisel, whose role resembles that of the narrator in Diego de San Pedro's *Carcel de Amor* (Prison of Love).[49] It is worth noting that Delicado's intervention in *Lozana* as a "guide" to the reader and as a friend and confidant of the protagonist might have also been inspired by a similar role of Felisel in *Question of Love* or by the earlier example of the author's intervention in the *Prison of Love*.

The *Question of Love* is rich in graphic descriptions of places and of several social events. The striking feature of this novel is that its descriptions resemble items "from a society chronicle or the jottings down of a memorandum book";[50] in fact, Flamiano, one of the characters of the novel, actually tells his chamberlain that he will give him the description of certain costumes that he has jotted in a *memorial* ("memorandum book").[51] This reference to the "memorandum book" along with the meticulously delineated episodic scenes, the portrayal of contemporary customs, and the accurate mention of historical events, is likely to have served as a model for Delicado's use of the *cuaderno* ("notebook", XVIII. 87), and his close adherence to reality.

At the threshold of the Renaissance the imitation of reality was encouraged also by Spanish moralists, among them Juan Luis Vives and Juan de Valdés, who praised the imitation of reality, seen as divine creation, and despised with few exceptions works of fiction, considered as elements of human vainglory.[52] Furthermore, the "literature of truth" was given a new impetus by the writers of the *comedias a noticia* ("plays about real things") which, according to Bartolomé de Torres Naharro, are based on "things noted and seen in the reality of the truth." Torres Naharro made this observation in the preface to his collected plays which were published under the title of *Propaladia*[53] (First Fruits of Pallas, Naples, 1517). Some of the plays in this collection reflect Naharro's own sensibility to realistic literature. Two plays in particular, the *Comedia Soldadesca* and *Tinelaria*, offer us a gallery of characters taken from real life and real circumstances: soldiers, officials, and servants are depicted in a direct and vivid style, as they struggle, suffer, and live in a world of thievery and vice in sixteenth-century Rome.[54]

The dramatic creations of Naharro must have been known to Delicado; he was certainly very familiar with the *Tinelaria*, which he praises, and from which he takes a character for his *Lozana*. And, furthermore, Delicado's thoughts on Rome and its inhabitants are almost identical to those expressed in the play (XLVIII, 190 ff).[55] Strikingly similar also are *Lozana*'s final pages and one of Torres Naharro's other works, a poem entitled the *Concilio de los galanes y cortesanas de Roma, invocado por Cupido* (Council of the Lovers and Courtesans of Rome, Called by Cupid, 1515?). The *Council* first complains of the spread of sodomy, then decrees that this and the lustful conduct of the courtesans be reformed. Later, courtesans are reprimanded for causing harm and evil. And, in a moralizing fashion, there is expressed concern for the fate of Rome. The vision of the profligate Roman life and the moralizing tone of the *Council* make it, in general terms, one of the most interesting precedents of Delicado's work, while the rhetorical style of the poem and the magisterial function of Cupido provide us with a very specific source for the Letter of excommunication, at the end of *Lozana*. Delicado, like Naharro, was intimately acquainted with the Roman society of his times, with the heterogeneous conglomeration of its people and their libertinism. What the author of *Lozana* probably marveled at and took as a model in the dramatist's representation of that society was Naharro's "dexterity in managing a scene of such turbulence and apparent confusion with such perfect control."[56]

In addition to *Celestina, Question of Love* and the works of Torres Naharro, there are other writings of the Renaissance which possibly served as literary models for *Lozana*. These are the *Cancionero de obras de burlas provocantes a risa* (Songbook of Burlesque Works that Provoke Laughter, Valencia, 1519), and two humanistic comedies, published jointly, *Thebaida* and *Serafina* (Valencia, 1521). *The Songbook of Burlesque Works* deals, in part, with the life of procuresses in the midst of prostitution in Valencia. A portion of this book, entitled the *Coplas de Fajardo* (Couplets of Fajardo), is mentioned in *Lozana* as another literary composition enjoyed by the protagonist (XLVII, 190).[57]

As for the comedies, on the other hand, they are not referred to specifically in *Lozana,* but each play could have been, nevertheless, a model or partial model for Delicado's work. Franquila, the young, beautiful, and lascivious protagonist in *Thebaida,* has been considered a direct model of Lozana. Her astuteness, ingenuity, and cynicism are fundamental qualities of Delicado's protagonist. Franquila's encounter with the pageboy Aminthas and the subsequent amorous scene have interesting similarities with the meeting of Lozana and Rampín and the love episode that follows. Whatever "obscenity" exists in this and other scenes, the *Thebaida* is clearly "intended to be funny, and not pornographic,"[58] and this is a lesson which Delicado applied to his own comic representation of sexual activity. In this respect, the only difference between *Thebaida* and *Lozana* is that in the latter, the humorous treatment of concupiscence is combined with a moral didactic purpose.

There is a strong possibility that Delicado also knew the comedy *Serafina,* a work which vividly describes popular manners and customs of sixteenth-century Spain. *Lozana's* affinity to *Serafina* can be seen not only in the realistic vision of life which it projects, but also in the use of a number of proverbial phrases and familiar terms that appear in the earlier work. And in two cases, in memoranda II and XII of *Lozana,* the protagonist and the washerwoman present an amusing enumeration of culinary specialities which, as we mentioned earlier, has a distinct similarity to that given by Arthemis in *Serafina*.[59]

VI Conclusion

In view of the above considerations, it is apparent that Delicado was very conscious of literary tradition and that his *Lozana* is not a negative and isolated product of Spanish letters without literary precedents, as Menéndez Pelayo believed,[60] but rather an artistic creation of considerable literary background. Several situations, characters, ideas, phrases, and terms that appear in *Lozana* have been shown to be imitations and elaborations of similar aspects in other works. The genius of Delicado lies in his ability to assimilate a variety of literary forms and concepts and to apply them creatively to a meaningful portrayal of the historical reality of his times.

CHAPTER 4

Delicado's role in Lozana

IN some forms of novelistic fiction the author serves the dual role of omniscient author-narrator and character. In such cases, he is often a friend or an admirer of the main character. The fictional starting point is supplied by the narrator's desire to describe the whole, or parts of, the life of the main protagonist or to depict experience which he has had in common with this great or interesting personality.[1]

I *Delicado as Author*

Lozana is an eminent example of a novel in which the author is both the omniscient narrator and a character in his work. In parts of the novel, Delicado-author assumes the point of view of limited omniscience, being intimately cognizant of Lozana only, not of all of the characters. Consistent with his artistic goal, the author's employment of the more restricted point of view is more likely to produce the illusion of life, as Clayton Hamilton suggests: "In actual experience, we see only one mind internally, — our own; all other people we look upon externally: and a story, therefore, which lays bare to us one mind and only one is more in tune with life itself than a story in which many minds are searched by one and all-seeing eye."[2]

In the Dedication, Delicado begins by expressing his desire to make his patron aware of the life and amorous exploits of the famous Lozana. In order to place the events of his protagonist immediately before the reader, Delicado has to provide a definite point in time and space. Accordingly, in the Dedication and in the accompanying Plot summary, the author-narrator proceeds to give background information concerning Renaissance Rome, the setting of his portrait, and Lozana, the exuberant Andalusian woman. Furthermore, he reveals the particular character of his portrait which he says is based only on things which he has "heard and seen" (p. 33). In this respect,

Delicado also indirectly fulfills the requirement cited by Bertil Romberg that "the narrator must consciously or unconsciously give a view of himself coming from 'within' the novel."[3]

Following the Dedication and the Plot summary Delicado, as omniscient author, opens the work proper by relating more details of Lozana's background and personality. Having presented the reader with a basic characterization of Lozana, the author moves temporarily aside and the novel begins to unfold in a series of dialogues, which provide us with successive details of time, place, and character. Periodically, however, the dialogues are supported by the narrator with summaries of events and descriptions of the protagonist's reflections and motivations. In this capacity the author acts as commentator for the reader.

The first time the author reappears as narrator is in memorandum IV, where he sums up the reflections and events following Lozana's encounter with Diomedes: their amorous sentiments, journeys to various Mediterranean cities, and tragic separation. Like the epic poet Ludovico Ariosto, Delicado guides the reader from one major scene to another, summarizing the events in between. In the following memorandum the author narrates Lozana's arrival in Rome, and he gives a concise report of her initial reaction and activities in the Eternal City. Interested in conveying a sense of the reality of all that he depicts, the author-narrator skillfully renders the thoughts, emotions, and actions of his protagonist. To enhance the effect of reality the author tries to make the reader a witness to the action, by addressing himself directly to the reader with such phrases as "And you should observe that she surpassed all these women . . ." (V, 47). The artistic technique of involving the reader in the narration had also been employed by the epic writers of the Middle Ages, to give a sense of truth and actuality to their poems. Moreover, like the medieval poets, Delicado uses the technique to sustain the reader's attention in the subject matter by promising that there are more delightful episodes to come, for example, by use of the phrase "as we shall see later" (V, 46).

In memorandum XIV Delicado appears as the spectator to a scene in which Rampín is awakened by the snoring Lozana. Still occupying a position of narrator the author contemplates the scene and he expresses his desire to sketch it: "I wish I knew how to describe a few snores . . ." (p. 76). Here Delicado appears as the self-conscious author aware of himself as a scrupulous writer. His account of Lozana's life and of the world around her must be like a chronicle recording the full range of experiences, and for this he strives to take note of the most minute details. In the same memorandum, Delicado-author also makes his presence felt in a series of digressions, in the form of a parenthesis or an aside, intended to place in a chronological framework the bedroom episode between Lozana and Rampín. In the middle of the scene, the author intervenes and says, "A short distance away there lived a smith who got up at midnight, and didn't let them sleep" (p. 77). Later the author intervenes again to inform the reader that "it was noon when the aunt came to awaken them . . ." (p. 77). Delicado-author also intrudes into the story to clarify a particular point. When in one instance Lozana makes a cryptic statement to Rampín about "that which will not permit me to sleep," the omniscient author appears again to inform the reader: "And she pointed to the wine bottle" (p. 77).

Fundamentally, the intrusion of Delicado-author in the novel is to summarize and explain the events taking place. Because of his preoccupation with the way the reader interprets the course of events laid before him, Delicado-author insists time and again that his chronicle is based only on the reality around him. This is reflected, for example, in his reference to *Lozana* as a "history composed in portrait form" (LXVI, 245). In the Apology his sentiments toward the work as a faithful portrait of reality are expressed once again. There he answers anticipated questions about his familiarity with the subject matter being portrayed: "If they should ask me how I managed to know so many intimate particulars, good or bad, I say that it is not difficult to write once what I have seen done and I have heard said so many times" (p. 248). The author-narrator's emphasis, at the end of the work, as at the beginning, is clearly on his audiovisual experiences, a technique which is designed to enhance the credibility of his report.

II *Delicado as Character*

Delicado's role in *Lozana* takes on a new dimension in memorandum XVII. The heading of this memorandum is significant: "Information which the author intercalates in order that what follows may be better understood." The "information" reveals that the author enjoys an intimate relationship with his characters, whose activities he jots down in a memorandum book. Now Delicado appears as the author and as a character in *Lozana:* "While writing the previous chapter, I felt a pain in my foot, and I put this notebook on the table, and there entered Rampín, who said 'what testament is this?' "

(XVII, 87). What we learn in memorandum XVII is that the author carefully records the events in the lives of others as well as the circumstances in his own life. From an omniscient commentator on the events in Lozana's life he now becomes an active participant in the action he is describing. The author reveals a personal knowledge of his protagonists. He asks Rampín, "Didn't I meet you at the time of Julius II, in Plaza Nagona, when you were serving a cleric?" (XVII, 89); and shortly afterwards he tells him, ". . . there I saw you stealing something. . . ." The author-character also begins to display an intimate concern for those around him. On the way out of the house, the author reminds Rampín that the staircase is dangerous; Rampín falls from the staircase and the author queries, "Did you hurt yourself?" (XVII, 91). Here the author becomes totally incorporated in the novel-portrait he is trying to create. In fact, the purpose of Rampín's visit is to invite the author to Lozana's house where, he is told, he will meet some beautiful courtesans. The author, however, declines the invitation for fear that he will be criticized for going around Rome with pen and paper ready to jot down details of places and people. His anticipated criticism is in itself revealing. As Professor Wardropper has noted, Delicado's art requires precisely that he follow Lozana through the streets of Rome, that he walk with her and look at her every move, recording everything he sees.[4] In the process of following Lozana through Rome the author will become personally involved with her and with the libertine world which surrounds them, as we shall soon see. The result is that he, like his characters, contracts venereal disease, suffers extensively as a consequence of his wanton life, and at the end recognizes the folly of human vanity.

In chapter 6 we will learn that the author records the events of the world around him not merely to produce an historical chapter on Renaissance Rome but also to teach a moral lesson, as he states in the preliminary pages. Accordingly, Rampín's reference to the author's notebook as a "testament" is highly symbolic. Theologically, "testament" refers to the promises of God as revealed in the Scriptures. Among these promises is the declaration that the just will be rewarded and the corrupt will be punished. An example of Divine punishment which Delicado recalls in the pages of *Lozana* is the destruction of Sodom and Gomorrah. The biblical event (Gen. 18,19) impressed itself deeply upon later generations as a warning of God's total judgment upon appalling wickedness. Delicado's "notebook" records events analogous to those of the biblical cities.

The licentiousness of Roman society is accompanied by physical suffering and followed by the plundering of Rome during the sack of 1527, seen by the author as divine punishment. In this respect *Lozana* becomes an exemplary "testament."

In memorandum XXIV the author again is seen directly involved with his characters, this time with Silvio, the servant of a Milanese gentleman. Silvio is watching Lozana walking when the author appears. He points her out to the author who, impressed by Lozana's beauty, insists on meeting her. Silvio and the author approach Lozana and they converse with her. Thus begins the author's personal acquaintance with the exuberant Andalusian woman. The author-character relationship with Lozana is seen developing in the next memorandum where there is recorded "how the author, a few days later, found Lozana in the house of his favorite courtesan and talked with her" (XXV, 121). The brief conversation that ensues increases the author's interest in Lozana, whom he will follow assiduously. The author's task of producing a truthful portrait is complicated by the mobility of the model, Lozana.[5] However, he persists in his endeavor and, in memorandum XLII, the reader is told "how Lozana being alone, . . . the author entered quietly, and the two debated" (p. 174). Their conversation discloses that the author has sought Lozana's services as a go-between, a fact that underlines even more his total participation in the world which he portrays. We also learn that, consistent with her intention of getting all that she can from her suitors and clients, Lozana has extorted money from the author as well. The author, of course, does not mind since he has found in this experience another of his protagonist's ingenious traits to be recorded.[6]

In the manner described above, Delicado as author-character proceeds to execute his portrait of Lozana with the greatest concern. He speaks to Lozana and he inquires about her. In memorandum XLIII we see the author standing at the front door of Lozana's house talking to several characters that are about to visit the Andalusian woman. He converses with Jacomina, a maid who brings food to Lozana, to a peasant who brings onions, and to Victoria, who has come to seek a cure for her painful womb. To Victoria the author makes specific inquiries into Lozana's method of dealing with the problem, and he is given a concise report of the treatment. Then he stops Penacho, a cleric's servant, who is leaving Lozana's house with some medication to treat the Monsignor's hemorrhoids. There too a conversation develops. The effect created by these conversations is that of showing the author in recognizable relation with his subject matter; thus, as Percy Lubbock observes, no question of his authority can arise.[7]

The preceding conversations elucidate the author's novelistic technique. Like a modern journalist, the author follows his subject, interviews those involved with it, and jots down all the particulars pertaining to it. The result in *Lozana* is that we not only see a world being portrayed, we also see the artist's hand while it is actually at work. Note the way in which the author-character shows himself at work. He tells Rampín, "Bring me some paper and ink, for I want to make a note here of something I have just remembered" (XLII, 176). Accordingly, the portrait is to be shown to us in its making, an artistic device of the artist for giving his work a greater appearance of truth. After all, as Joyce Cary has pointed out, it is every novelist's goal "to try to convey reality — the fact plus the feeling, a total complex experience of a real world."[8]

As we indicated earlier, the author's intention in portraying Lozana's life and that of the Roman world is linked to his desire to teach a moral lesson. The author's intervention in his work offers the advantage of moralizing directly to his characters. To his friend Silvio, who has informed him of Lozana's deceptions, the author-character remarks: "Oh what a bad woman! Why don't they whip her?" (XXIV, 116). Then he addresses himself to Lozana and says, "They should cover your head with a criminal's cap" (XXIV, 117). When he is told about Lozana's occult practices the author states, "In Spain such superstitions would never be tolerated" (XXIV, 120). Later, the author-character reprimands Lozana and the other courtesans for their worldliness: "You should know that for the most part, all of you are inclined more to evil and envy than you are to good" (XLII, 177). These statements show that there is a basic inconsistency in the author's role in the work. He is both an active participant in that libertine life and a censurer of its evils. As Professor Díez Borque has indicated, this fundamental dualism in the author-character participation in, and aversion to, the world which is being portrayed reminds us of a similar technique found in *Guzmán de Alfarache*.[9] There, Guzmán, the protagonist, is alternately a sinful pícaro and a profound sermonizer. As sermonizer, Guzmán, however, accuses others of transgressing God's law, but not himself. Professor McGrady elucidates this point by citing Guzmán's statement when describing the perversity of his first wife: "And I may truly confesse unto you, that in all that time that I lived with her, I cannot accuse my selfe, nor did shee ever tax me of any the least injury that I had done her...."[10] This is not so in the case of Delicado-character. Intervening in the work as actor-sermonizer, Delicado also includes himself among those who have disobeyed the law of God. Thus, in memorandum XXIV, the author-character prognosticates to Silvio the future destruction of Rome as divine punishment for the sins of its inhabitants. Since it is clear that the author, too, has partaken in their sinful conduct, he admits, implicitly, his guilt and a partial responsibility for that punishment. Although there are notable differences in the structure of *Lozana* and *Guzmán*, the basic sinner-moralizer dualism of the author-character in one case, and of the protagonist in the other, is analogous in both works.

III Conclusion

In conclusion, *Lozana* is a novel in which the author not only relates and interprets his subject matter from a position of limited omniscience but, as a character, he is also an active part of the world he depicts. Actually, the two functions of the author complement each other. Delicado-author and narrator gives a pictorial description of his subject matter while Delicado-character, the dramatized author, shows how the literary portrait is being made. Like Diego de San Pedro, Velázquez, and Cervantes, the author of *Lozana* observes the world of his portrait from an internal perspective, thereby bringing realism into greater relief. Professors Prieto and Díez Borque have clarified this point.[11] Díez Borque has noted, for example, that in the beginning of chapter 10, Part II, of *Quijote,* Cervantes displays a concern for his protagonist's fate and an investigative attitude toward his work that brings to mind Delicado's role in *Lozana.* Prieto's comments on Cervantes's multiple points of view are clearly applicable to Delicado: "Cervantes frequently appears in his work, speaking about his own book, about his problems as a novelist, about himself and the transcendence of his creation."[12] Aside from giving his portrait a greater precision and individuality, Delicado's intervention in his work provides very useful information about his life and habits; it also shows the notable extent to which his life is linked to the world he portrays. Finally, the author's intervention as a character in his work makes his obviously didactic intention more meaningful, since he, too, becomes the object of moral judgment.

CHAPTER 5

The Historicity of Lozana

I *Introduction*

TOWARD the end of the fifteenth century, during the pontificates of Calixtus III and Alexander VI, Rome came to be, among other things, a center of libertinism. It is not surprising, therefore, that all those searching for worldly pleasures gathered there. It should also be recalled that the great exodus of Spanish Jews, fleeing from religious persecution, took place at this same time and that they found refuge in Rome, too. Among them was Francisco Delicado, the future author of *Lozana,* a work which reflects the world of Renaissance Rome in an extraordinary way.

As is known, there exists (or at least there existed until recently) a conspiracy of silence caused by the exaggerated puritanical criticism which saw in *Lozana* a parade of sinners and pornographic scenes.[1] Nevertheless, since the discovery of this work, in the nineteenth century, the same criticism vaguely mentions its importance as a primary source for a depiction of the social atmosphere and customs of Renaissance Rome. In addition to its literary and artistic importance and its similarity to the celestinesque novel and the picaresque genre, *Lozana* stands out by virtue of its descriptions of the epoch, its gallery of vivid characters, and its popular image of Rome. It is, thus, a magnificent historical document which forms an integral part of the difficult and complex discussion of modern Spanish history.[2] The purpose of this chapter is to document a valuable historical aspect of the work.

II *The Courtesans*

One social segment of Roman life which the author saw and knew very well is that of the courtesans. The first mention of the courtesans in *Lozana* is found in memorandum XII, in which Rampín shows the recently arrived Lozana around the city (XII, 62):

[47]

Rampín: Along this street we will find as many courtesans together as bees in a hive.
Lozana: And which ones are they?
Rampín: We will see them at the jalousied windows.

Later, another character, Divicia, also a courtesan, estimates how many of these women are in Rome when she says to Lozana: "I will tell you how many I know. There are thirty thousand whores and nine thousand bawds, not counting you" (LIV, 211). Although Divicia's statement is not to be taken literally, let us note, nevertheless, that according to the *Diario* (Diary) of Esteban Infessura, the number of such courtesans, at the end of the fifteenth century, reached 7,000,[3] in a population of Rome which was less than 50,000. Actually, there must have been so many women in Renaissance Rome who dedicated themselves to the low life, that when Pope Pius V wanted to evict them from the city, he had to give up the idea since the number of people who might have left would have exceeded twenty-five thousand.

Who were these courtesans to whom Rampín and Divicia refer? According to Lozana's interpretation, these women must have represented the aristocracy of strumpets, and therefore they came to be called "honest strumpets." Lozana says it when she exclaims: "The Roman women are right; there are not more chaste or honest women than they in the world" (XLVIII, 192). Lozana's view of the Roman courtesans as "chaste" and "honest" women concurs with that of the historian Giovanni Burcardo when he refers to "A certain courtesan that is an honest strumpet."[4] It must be remembered, of course, that "honest" in the classical meaning of the word did not imply sexual morality, but rather social nobility and decorum.[5]

The manner in which these courtesans distinguished themselves from the others is expressed by one of the characters of *Lozana*, the mail carrier, when he answers the young Cordovan lady's question (XX, 100): "What is the difference between rich courtesans and poor ones? Are they whores of political factions or of the world?"

Mail carrier: They are all whores; I don't know how to explain the difference to you except that there are whores by nature, and ones who were forced to it, that is, obliged by circumstances, and there are whores behind jalousied windows.

The latter women, the mail carrier explains, have wax-covered sheets at their windows, and they are held in great esteem. "There are others who put small rugs at their windows and they are even more famous"; these, he adds, "show all of themselves and are greatly admired by the gallants" (XX, 101). Such a distinction of the Roman courtesans concurs with what Armellini records in his census of Rome under the pontificate of Pope Leo X.[6] It is necessary to note, nevertheless, that the system of applying qualifying names to designate the type of courtesan was not very uniform and, therefore, of little historical value, as Gnoli indicates: "The different names [of the courtesans] which are found in the *Census* of Armellini do not have great value, considering that the census of the different parishes was made by different persons. They change names according to the persons who made the compilations."[7]

Well documented, however, is the libertinesque atmosphere of the famous districts of Pozo Blanco, Ponte Sisto, Campo de Flor, and Plaza Navona, in which the courtesans of *Lozana* practiced their arts.[8] Lozana's life in her first days in Rome unfolds in the district called Pozo Blanco,[9] where she finds many of her compatriots, with whom she converses about Roman life and shares her knowledge of culinary and cosmetic preparations (V - XI).

Lozana's finding several Spaniards in Pozo Blanco's relaxed atmosphere is explained by the historical fact that around 1456 the Spanish cardinal Rodrigo Borja, after having been named vice-chancellor, had established himself there, forming a Spanish colony composed in general of church functionaries, artisans, and shirtmakers. The women associated with these men led, for the most part, a licentious life.[10] It is there, in one of the most colorful and famous districts of Renaissance Rome, that Lozana, young and deprived of a means of livelihood in her completely new world, realizes the necessity to exploit her natural talents. With the help of some Spanish chambermaids, the recently arrived woman begins to profit from her astuteness and her knowledge of medical and magical arts. It is interesting to note that among the chambermaids whom Lozana finds there are Mencia and Beatriz, who appear in Armellini's *Census* under the names "Madonna Menzia Aloysia" and "Beatrice Yspana."[11]

According to history, Pozo Blanco was a district in the Parione area of Rome, seemingly very well-known and populated by Spaniards. In his edition of *Propaladia,* Joseph Gillet says: "It was a place well-known to Spaniards, since Alonso Enrique de Guzmán (Vida, 23), soon after arriving in Rome, about 1520, set out 'for Pozo Blanco, for I had often heard it mentioned.' "[12] Actually, Pozo Blanco was a very famous zone on account of the great number of courtesans who were living there; Gnoli, in his city census, estimates the population at 1,500, that is, three percent of the total population of Rome.[13] Maria Teresa Russo suggests the bad reputation Pozo Blanco had at the beginning of the sixteenth century when she speaks of the allusion to the district made next to the description of the 1625 plan of Rome: "The area around this church [Santa Maria Vallicella] was many years ago a public brothel, hence when they wanted to exaggerate an infamous thing, they said 'This was never done in Pozzo Bianco!' "[14]

The second stage of Lozana's life in Rome begins when the pretty Cordovan is directed to the Neapolitan lady, owner of a cosmetic shop and mother of Rampín, in the eleventh memorandum of the novel. The next memorandum records the way the pícaro Rampín enters the service of the delightful Lozana, whom he serves well by guiding her through the brothel-like atmosphere of the Eternal City (XII, 61):

Lozana: Do one thing, my dear. That is, no matter where we go, be sure to tell me about each thing there and what the streets are called.
Rampín: This is the Ceca, where money is made; and here's where you go to Campo de Flor and to the Colosseum; and over here is the bridge....

Later, Rampín will accompany Lozana to Campo de Flor, but now they stop, though briefly, on what Rampín calls the bridge, that is, Ponte Sisto, the famous bridge and district of Rome where Lozana sees several courtesans. Noting the presence of one of these women, a conversation ensues (XII, 63):

Lozana: And who is that lady from Andorra who is wearing a hat, and moves her hips well, and is accompanied by two young servant girls?
Rampín: That one? Oh, she is one of the dear courtesans from around here. Look what a multitude of them go by there! They seem like a swarm of bees, and the courtiers follow them. At this time of day they go out dressed in disguise.

Although Ponte Sisto, as Pozo Blanco and Campo de Flor, was famous for the tricksters, charlatans, and bankers who gathered there, it was even more famous for being one of the largest centers of courtesans.[15] Rampín's reference to the multitude of courtesans concurs with the historical documentation which we have of Ponte Sisto, as the neighborhood where there was a lot of activity on the part of the courtesans, usually of the lowest class.[16]

From Pozo Blanco and Ponte Sisto, Rampín accompanies Lozana to another renowned site in Rome, Plaza Navona. "This is called Nagona," Rampín points out; "and if you come here on Wednesday, you will find the most organized and orderly market you will probably ever see in your whole life. . . . There is nothing that grows on earth or lives in the sea which is not there. . . ." And, later, after seeing some courtesans and their lovers, Rampín explains to Lozana: " . . . those are courtesans, and those men must be important nobles" (XV, 81).

Despite the fact that Plaza Navona is a huge commercial center, as Rampín points out and as history attests,[17] it is interesting to note the presence of the courtesans even in this principal marketplace of the city. According to Delicado's work, these women are actually found everywhere in Rome, a fact documented by the historians Armellini and Domenico Gnoli.[18]

The omnipresence of the courtesans in Renaissance Rome, seen here mainly in Rampín and Lozana's tour through three of the most famous neighborhoods of the city, is accompanied by much information concerning their way of life. In memorandum XXII, Trigo, the Jew, says to Lozana: "Señora, I have found you a house belonging to a rich woman who has been a courtesan . . . and is served by slaves like a queen" (p. 107). Later Lozana will tell us: "[In Rome] there is no courtesan, no matter how low she may be, who does not have her palace servant" (XXXIV, 147). Lozana again refers to the good living of many Roman courtesans when, visiting in the home of the Garza Montesina, she distinguishes Clarina and Madam Aviñonesa among the courtesans of the time, for their grace, splendor, great luxury, and wealth (LVIII, 222).[19] In short, forty-six courtesans are mentioned or appear in Delicado's work, spending their fortunes and that of their friends on luxuries. "They meet to talk, to eat, and to dance," observes Segundo Serrano Poncela; " . . . they stroll through the streets followed by pages and servants; [and] they seem to enwrap the city with their breath, splendorous robes, and gaiety."[20] The description of the luxury and opulence which characterize the life of the Roman courtesans in Delicado's novel has historic parallels in the work of the sixteenth-century Italian writer Cesare Vecellio. He speaks about the excessive elegance of the Renaissance courtesan: "They used very fine white, perfumed clothes, dresses of silk, velvet and richly gilded silks, pompous attire, the most rare furs, gloves tanned with Spanish jasmine or carnations, lace and precious pendants from Venice; they dazzled with their rings, bracelets, fancy collars, earrings, and diadems."[21]

The Roman courtesans displayed such elegance and luxury not only in their dress, but also in their homes, where they lived surrounded by maidservants, as Lozana reveals. This aspect of the courtesans' life is discussed also by contemporaries of Delicado, such as Niccolò Franco[22] and Matteo Bandello,[23] and more recently by the historian Arturo Graf. Upon considering the many works written on this aspect of Roman life, Graf deduces that the rooms of the courtesans must have been worthy of princesses and that their houses were provided with several maidservants and pages.[24]

In conclusion, Delicado shows a profound knowledge of Renaissance Roman life. His manner of describing that world and portraying those who lived in it impresses us with its historical fidelity. Before and after Delicado, other writers had been in contact with the same Roman scene, and through them, as Alfonso Reyes notes, "that social awakening, that sensuous kiss of Renaissance Rome have reached literature."[25] Nevertheless, the outstanding aspect of Delicado's art is the singular realism with which he depicts that Roman world dominated by an attitude of shamelessness and freedom, as expressed by Lozana: "I would like fear and shame to be lost in my lifetime so that each one may seek and do whatever he pleases" (LXII, 235). Actually, as Graf notes, that was the spirit of sixteenth-century Italy. That spirit undoubtedly contributed to social disintegration and corruption and to the rise in popularity of the courtesans, as well as to their libertinism and opulence, to such an extent that Rome, the seat of Christendom, became, in Rampín's words: " . . . the triumph of the grandees, the paradise of whores, the purgatory of young people, the hell of all, the weariness of beasts, the cheater of the poor, the fishpond of rascals and criminals . . . " (XV, 81). This view of the Eternal City would be sadly confirmed three years later, in 1527, by Alfonso de Valdés: "My heart was saddened to see that city (which rightfully should be an example of virtue to everyone) so filled with vice, deceptions, and open roguery."[26]

III *The* mal francés

The account which Delicado gives of the free and libertine life of the courtesans in Renaissance Rome and of the licentious world in which they lived is historically well related with the plague of the time, the *mal francés* ("French disease," syphilis). Delicado's knowledge of this disease was personal and profound, as we can see from the two tracts he wrote about its treatment. In *Lozana,* the first reference made to *mal francés* occurs in memorandum XII, in which Lozana asks the washerwoman: "Tell me, how long have you been in

Rome?" (p. 66), and the washerwoman answers: "Since the disease came here from France . . . ," which Delicado states, some pages later, had its beginning in the year 1488 (LIII, 202).

The origin of this social plague is still unknown, although there was already talk about *mala franzos (mal francés)* in 1472. It must be noted, however, that the date which Delicado gives us coincides with the mention made of this disease by Peter Mártir of Anglería in a letter written in 1488 to his friend Arias Barbosa.[27] In it Mártir sympathizes with his friend's suffering from what the Spaniards called *bubas* ("syphilitic pustules") and the Italians *morbus gallicus* ("Gallic disease," "venereal disease"). According to Delicado, this disease had its origin in Naples in 1488, and its spread was due to the dissolute lives of the soldiers of Charles VIII during his campaign to capture the kingdom of Naples. The courtesan Divicia says in memorandum LII of *Lozana:* " . . . when King Charles came to Naples, the incurable disease began . . . " (p. 202). This coincides with what Delicado tells us in another work of his, *El modo de adoperare el legno de India occidentale* (On the Use of the West Indies' Wood), a treatise written for the purpose of alleviating the suffering of those who, like him, had been victims of this disease.

Nevertheless, we should note that while the Italians believed the French responsible for the disease, and therefore called it "Gallic disease," the French, thinking they had contracted it in Naples, called it *mal de Nápoles* ("Neapolitan disease"),[28] and the disease subsequently acquired other names as well. Speaking of the tendency to blame this disease on others, Fernán Xuárex observed in 1548: "Each nation blames it on the foreigners. The French call it the Spanish disease, the Spaniards the French affliction, and others call it the disease from the Indies."[29]

Much was written about this disease in Europe toward the end of the fifteenth century and during the sixteenth.[30] As we have noted, its name varied quite a bit, so that in *Lozana* it is called *mal de Francia, mal francorum, mal de Nápoles, mal incurable* and *mal del greñimón* or *griñimón*. With regard to the last name of the disease, Puyol y Alonso observed: " . . . We don't know what the word *grillimón, grilimón, greñimón,* or *griñimón* specifically meant, for it was said in four ways, seemingly; but, we suspect that it must be a popular term used to describe the alopecia of the eyebrows resulting from venereal disease. . . . "[31] What is known is that the name *grillimón* and its variants for denoting the "French disease" existed already at the end of the fifteenth century.

Grillimón as a synonym for venereal disease appears also in some interesting verses of the sixteenth-century Toledan writer Sebastián de Horozco.[32] In his *Cancionero,* Horozco refers to the ailment with cynicism and humor, as *santo grillimón* ("holy grillimón"), in one instance mocking a syphilitic man who has become bald. As far as it is known, the cause and effect relationship between venereal disease and loss of hair appears for the first time in *Lozana* (VI, 48), and it is reiterated in a satirical novel of the seventeenth century entitled, *La pícara Justina* (Justina: The Country Jilt).[33] A recent study by Jack Weiner[34] has shown that the frequently ironic and burlesque usage of *grillimón,* as it appears in *Lozana* and in Horozco's poem, can be explained by the etymological association with the word *greña* ("entangled or matted hair"). "Calling a syphilitic man *greñudo,* for being bald, would obviously be a cruel way of ridiculing him."[35] Significantly, Weiner has also discussed the possibility that, at least in Horozco's case, *grillimón* carries the additional association with the word *grillos* ("shackles or chains for the feet"; "any impediment which prevents motion"); the idea being that syphilis, like the chains, constrains mobility.[36]

Thus, the syphilitic victim was frequently mocked and considered helpless, since the efforts made to cure the disease gave little results. This is documented in the pages of the *Historia bibliográfica de la medicina española* (Bibliographical History of Spanish Medicine), by Hernández Morejón,[37] and it is perceived also in *Lozana* where this effort is considered not only futile but ridiculous. In memorandum LIX, Lozana tells the surgeon: " . . . there isn't so stupid a doctor as the one who wants to cure the *griñimón*" (p. 226). Despite this sense of futility, Delicado himself wrote two treatises offering his beliefs concerning the disease and its cure: the already mentioned *On the Use of the West Indies' Wood* and *On Consoling the Infirm.* Of these two treatises, only the first has survived, that is, the one dealing with the West Indies' wood. The description of the "French disease" and its origin found in this treatise concurs with that given in *Lozana.* In memorandum LIV of Delicado's novel, the courtesan Divicia explains that, finally, the great plague began to diminish by means of the wood from the Indies. In this, Delicado testifies to the veracity of the wood's curative properties, as does Gonzalo Fernández de Oviedo, who writes about "the holy wood which the Indians call *guayacán* ['guaiacum']."[38] Parenthetically, it is interesting to note that, agreeing with the opinions of various natural historians of the sixteenth century, Delicado points out the island of Santo Domingo as the source of this wood and as the place where the natives had for some time cured themselves of various diseases with the boiled fruit and wood of this tree.

In *Lozana* little is said about the treatment for curing the affliction, though much is reported of its origin, as we have noted, and of the great suffering it caused. In any case, *Lozana* is historically important as one of the first documents furnishing evidence of the disasters caused by syphilis. In the words of Rafael Alberti it was a scourge "of the armies of the times, [of] the soldiers who fell wounded between the sheets rather than on the battlegrounds."[39] Of course, many others in Renaissance Rome became victims of this plague, especially the courtesans. In memorandum XXIV of *Lozana* the companion comments: "Women on this earth . . . are subject to three things: to the house rent, to gluttony, and to the disease which afterwards comes to them from Naples . . . " (p. 114), an observation which is reminiscent of the adage which says: "Man who goes about the world, eats bread which is not fresh, sleeps on the ground, raises lice, itches and gets the French disease."[40] Lozana herself is no exception to this rule, since in the course of her vicissitudes she contracts the disease which leaves her marked for the rest of her life (VII, 49).

In view of the preceding discussion, it does not surprise us that *Lozana* should have been considered a daughter "born of life and not of books."[41] In nothing is this truer than in the worthy historical portrait which Delicado offers us of the happy, libertine world of the Renaissance courtesans and of the plague which destroyed their lives and the lives of those with whom they shared their passions. *"Lozana* makes us penetrate into a strange and singular world," said Menéndez Pelayo;[42] strange, yes, but also authentic, since it incarnates the materialism and the vitality of Renaissance Rome.

IV *Jews and* Conversos *in* Lozana

One of the most interesting aspects of Spain's social, political, and literary history is that which revolves around the Jews and their co-religionists who, for various motives, embraced the Catholic faith and became known as conversos or New Christians.[43]

Throughout the Spanish Middle Ages the Jews occupied a significant role in the social and intellectual activity of the country. They held important positions at court, became administrators of estates, architects, and doctors. And, ideologically, they perpetuated those moral and didactic teachings one finds in the Hebrew Wisdom literature.

At the threshold of the Renaissance, however, the role of the Jews in Spain began to deteriorate. After eight centuries of religious wars, Spain gained political unity under the Catholic monarchs, Ferdinand and Isabella (ruled jointly 1474 - 1504), whose desire for territorial unity as well as religious harmony led to the expulsion of nonconverted Jews and Moors, in 1492.

To test the religious integrity of those Jews and infidels who had become christianized and to safeguard against heresy, the Spanish Inquisition was established in 1479. Its proceedings were motivated not only by religious beliefs but also by political aims, and they were always conducted with great severity, especially during the first hundred years of its existence. The lengthy and extraordinary measures taken by the Inquisition to scrutinize the background and activities of the conversos led to an ever-increasing spirit of suspicion and prejudice against the New Christians, a fact which, in turn, resulted in a massive exodus of conversos to various parts of Europe, particularly to Italy.

The importance of *Lozana* as an historical document can be seen in yet another aspect of the work: the description of the conversos and their relationship with the Jews in Renaissance Rome.[44] Delicado, a converso, knew well the mentality, motivation, and life style of the New Christians, whose lives and customs he skillfully portrays in the pages of *Lozana*. As Professor Márquez Villanueva has shown, the author's consciousness of the social, human, and ideological traits of the New Christians is apparent from the beginning of the novel, in the characterization of the protagonist.[45] Consistent with the proverbial wisdom of those of Jewish blood,[46] the young Lozana is seen endowed with great sagacity, ingenuity, and shrewdness in practical affairs. References to the protagonist's talents and astuteness are frequent in the work. It is with pride that the author depicts Lozana as a natural and symbolic "compatriot of Seneca" for her intellect (I, 37), while he finds her "related to Ropero," the bold converso poet of the fifteenth century, for her eloquence and crafty art (XXXVI, 154).[47]

When the unfortunate outcome of her relationship with Diomedes, her lover, takes her to Rome, Lozana actively seeks companionship among conversos, in the Pozo Blanco district of Rome. This quarter of the city, like that of Plaza Navona, was known, as we have seen, for its population of courtesans, as well as for its converso community. It is in Pozo Blanco that Lozana begins to live by her wits and skills, thus making the earlier allusions to her ingenuity seem prophetic.

Lozana's first acquaintances in Rome are a few converso women, all Andalusians, a *camisera* ("shirtmaker") and her friends Teresa de Córdoba, Beatriz de Baeza, and Marina Hernández. Their surnames reveal converso affiliation, as can be seen, for example, in the frequency with which people by the name of Córdoba, Baeza, and Hernández appear in a financial transaction between King Ferdinand and the New Christians, in a document called the *Sevillian Composition of 1510*.[48] In addition, as Ruth Pike has observed, the trades of the shirtmaker and of her friends' husbands — moneychanger, linen merchant, and rag merchant — are also professions traditional among the conversos.[49] Their ancestors, the Jews, had been prominent in commerce since the Middle Ages, and equally old was their association with loan banks and pawnbroking. So active were the Jews in the business enterprise that as early as the tenth century "Jew" had become, even in legal terminology, a synonym for merchant.[50]

The characterization of Lozana's own converso background is strengthened when the Andalusian women of Pozo Blanco decide to put to a test their recently arrived compatriot. Their desire to "know from her if she is a converso, so that we could speak without fear" (VII, 51), leads them to ascertain whether Lozana will prepare a certain specialty, *hormigos* ("sweet fritters") with water or oil. Attempting to adhere to Jewish dietary laws, the conversos had traditionally included the use of oil in the preparation of the delicacies, and when Lozana tells the women that she will prepare the fritters with a lot of good olive oil, they rejoice, exclaiming: "For goodness sake, she is one of ours!" (VIII, 53). Lozana follows well her grandmother's way of preparing the *hormigos*, described in an earlier memorandum, and she thus passes the test.

The converso identity of Lozana and of those around her is reinforced by their contempt for pork, as can be seen from the companion's remark about Lozana: "If they do not please her, she will speak of them worse than of pork" (XXIV, 115).[51] Later, however, one of the characters, Falillo, alludes to the fact that the *tocino* ("bacon") was secretly used by many of those Spanish exiles (XXXIV, 149). And when the shrewd Lozana reaches the height of her material success in Rome, she openly discloses that her pantry abounds with *presutos* ("cured hams") and other pork delicacies. This fact, combined with various ironic religious references, characterizes the fundamentally ambivalent nature of Lozana, which is perceptively described by Teresa de Córdoba's remark, "I have a feeling that this Lozana will behave like a Christian, among Christians, like a Jew, among Jews, like a Turk, among Turks, like a noblewoman, among nobles . . . since for everyone she has a pretext" (IX, 56). In fact, as Francisco Márquez properly observes, Lozana's vacillation with respect to her attitudes and her indifference toward any organized religion is in itself a manifestation of her converso background, one which tended to perpetuate the shock of forced conversions.[52]

Continuing and relentless pressure from both Church and state to bring the reluctant Jews to the baptismal font had been applied since the early days of the Inquisition, whose goals were frequently attained through intimidation and violence. The ultimate effect of such traumatic exprreriences was that of creating an atmosphere of confusion and skepticism among the conversos. With *Lozana* herself, it is interesting to note, however, that ultimately the libertine protagonist does find a stabilizing force in the contemplation of the universal truth of human vanity and folly.

In his portrait of the conversos in *Lozana,* Delicado also treats their kinship with the Jews. In memorandum IX, Lozana inquires into the presence of Jews in Rome, and she is told by Beatriz not only that there are many but that they are also considered the New Christians' best friends (IX, 55).

Historically, the Expulsion Edict of Ferdinand and Isabella, signed on March 31, 1492, and made public between April 29 and May 1, compelled approximately 250,000 Jews to leave Spain.[53] So many of them sought asylum in Italy, and particularly in Rome, that a sixteenth-century chronicler reports that certain Roman Jews, "fearing that the influx would bring with it an outburst of anti-Semitism, requested the notorious Borgia Pope, Alexander VI, to exclude the refugees, supporting their petition with a gift of 1,000 ducats."[54] The Pope, however, in the true spirit of his noble office, declined the request and demanded instead another 2,000 ducats to allow the petitioners to remain. Whatever the truth of this report is, Cecil Roth observes that, in addition to the six old and established Italian congregations and those maintained by French and German immigrants, synagogues, following the Castilian, the Catalan, and the Aragonese . . . rites, were also established in Rome at that time.[55]

The rather favorable relationship which the neophytes enjoy with the Jews in *Lozana* reflects the historical fact that, to a considerable extent, many conversos often embraced their new faith only for the less than noble motives of saving their lives or improving their fortune. Their frequently superficial "conversion" explains their strong attachment to tradition and to the fact that many of them returned increasingly to their former faith.[56] Certainly, judging from Rampín's extensive familiarity with the Jewish quarter, his very strong aversion to pork, and Falillo's symbolic remark in which he plays with the words "God" and "baptism," in memorandum XXXIV, it appears that, consistent with the spirit of some of the characters in Delicado's work, they betray a very notable affinity with their former coreligionists.

When Lozana asks to be shown some of those Jews, Beatriz simply points to a group of individuals wearing a distinguishing mark (IX, 55). Indeed, the Jews living in Italy were required to exhibit a humiliating badge of shame to make them recognizable, first, in the shape of the Greek letter T (tau) and of a bluish color, and later in the form of a yellow or red circle.[57] They lived in segregated quarters, and each nationality group practiced the faith in different synagogues, which Rampín carefully enumerates in his tour of the *Juderia* ("the Jewish quarter") with Lozana.

The synagogues of Rome, like the Jewish communities of that city, were numerous, and several traced their origins to the earliest settlement of the Jews in Italy, probably around the second, or perhaps even the third century, before the beginning of the Christian era.[58] Now, as a result of the expulsion of 1492, they flourished, as can be seen from the fact that about a sixth of the Jews living in Italy at the beginning of the sixteenth century were concentrated in Rome.[59]

It is in the Jewish quarter that Lozana and Rampín meet the shrewd Trigo, an unscrupulous Jew who deals in everything from precious stones to clothing items, not to mention his involvement with the "well-being" of the notorious courtesans. Trigo first buys a precious ring which Rampín had found and quickly sells it to a silversmith, making a tidy profit for himself. Then he provides Lozana with fine clothing, which he had bought from the famous courtesan Imperia, and finally he supplies her with a furnished home, the rent of which he pays for six months so that Lozana can leisurely begin her career as a courtesan. The return for such services are clearly implied in Trigo's words that he will send the young woman those who will pay for her lodging as well as for her sustenance. "The good Jew," says Trigo, symbolically, "makes gold out of straw" (XVI, 85), and everything in the two memoranda in which he appears characterizes him as the proverbial Jew. Worth noting, in connection with Trigo's Jewishness, is an intentional reference which he makes to *Diô,* to avoid mentioning *Dios* ("God") (XVI, 84), which to the Jews appeared as a plural form proper to the Christian trinitarianism.[60]

The heterogeneous agglomeration of Jews living in Italy resulted frequently in bitter disputes between the foreign and Italian Jews, with a concomitant criticism of the latter, as the words of Rampín exemplify: "There is the synagogue of the Catalans . . . and there the synagogue of the Italians, who are the most foolish of all for trying to be like the gentiles while ignoring their own law" (XVI, 84). Rampín's critical attitude toward the Italian Jews stems probably from their well-known efforts to perpetuate their control of the community, a fact that would naturally make them seem more akin to the gentiles than to their coreligionists in the eyes of the Spanish Jews.

While denouncing the Italian Jews as hypocrites, Rampín praises the Spanish Jews for their intelligence and wisdom. "Our Spanish Jews," he remarks, "know more than all the others, for there are among them wise and wealthy men who are very learned" (XVI, 84). Within the context of sixteenth-century Rome, Rampín's remarks are clearly exaggerated, although historical documentation does reflect significant activity in artistic work and in the scientific inquiry and achievement among the Spanish Jews and conversos living in Renaissance Italy.[61]

Among the distinguished Spanish Jews living in Rome at that time was the playwright Solomon Usque, who translated Petrarch's sonnets into his native language and published an Italian poem on the Creation, which he dedicated to Cardinal Borromeo. Another outstanding member of the Jewish community of Italy was Joseph ha-Cohen, the physician, whose *Valley of Tears* is one of the best sources of Jewish history of the epoch. Wealthy and powerful families of Spanish origin — the Ascarelli, Ambrons, Corcos — also played a notable role in Roman communal life.[62]

Rampín's knowledge of the existence of "wise," "wealthy," and "very learned" Spanish Jews in sixteenth-century Italy is based, of course, on hearsay. Not so for Delicado, however, whose few but vivid sketches of the Jews and of the conversos reflect a keen sense of historical understanding and personal appreciation of their life and customs. Perceptively the author analyzes and exalts the shrewdness of those New Christians and Jews whose lives were

The Historicity of Lozana

directed to the enjoyment of life and to profit-making. From the social, psychological, and aesthetic point of view, the Jews and the conversos in *Lozana* present that blend of idealism and reality that is so notably inherent in their tradition.

CHAPTER 6

Meaning and Form of Lozana

IN the previous chapter we saw to what point *Lozana* is an important representation of the Roman Renaissance world, from the minutely detailed iconographic descriptions of the city to the portrait of its inhabitants profoundly involved in the pleasures of life. Wellek and Warren have pointed out that "literature 'represents life', and 'life' is, in large measure, a social reality;"[1] however, the eminent critics remind us that the studies which consider a novel as a mirror or a reproduction of life "only make sense if we know well the artistic method of the novelist being studied."[2] The purpose of this chapter is to analyze *Lozana* to show that it is not merely a social document or a scandalous work of an irregular and chaotic nature, as some critics would have us think,[3] but rather a carefully delineated literary portrait in which the organic elements create a contextual unity and a formal coherence which elucidates the moral and artistic intention of the author. "Analyzing a literary work," Joaquín Casalduero notes, "consists precisely in uncovering the functional symbolism of all the elements which constitute it, penetrating into it in depth."[4] To achieve these goals, it is necessary to analyze the form of *Lozana,* using the word in its Aristotelian sense; that is to say, form as it is constituted by the elements which determine the character, the meaning, and the special expression of the artistic creation, through the external and internal or narrative structure.[5]

I *Structure*

It is useful here to recall *Lozana*'s structural components: Dedication, Plot Summary, the First Part, with twenty-three *mamotretos* ("memoranda"), the Second Part, with forty-three memoranda, Apology, Explanation, Epilogue, Letter of excommunication, Lozana's Epistle, and author's Digression. In creating his novel, Delicado employs the technique of the literary portrait, confirmed by the title of the work, *Retrato de la Lozana andaluza* (Portrait of Lozana: The Exuberant Andalusian Woman). In the beginning of the First Part, the author refers to his work as a "history or portrait" and, in the last memorandum, he concludes, "May the history composed in portrait-form end."

The importance which Delicado attributes to the literary portrait as a vehicle for representing the world which surrounds him and the formal elements which he employs in his task as truthful artist, evident from the Dedication to the final pages of his work, provides us with the structural thread that gives unity to the work. Nothing better proves the importance of truth for Delicado's purpose than the Digression of *Lozana:* "Socrates is a friend, Plato is a friend, but truth is a better friend" (Digression, 259).[6] The result is a realistic literary portrait with an affinity to historic deeds and events. What we shall observe here is how that Roman world and its Renaissance spirit[7] come alive within the scheme of a literary portrait by means of a coherent structure, a narration in dialogue, and a lifelike style, and how the artistic form complements the moral meaning of the work.

In the Dedication of the work, Delicado introduces the principal elements of his portrait: Señora Lozana and the events of her time. Since "art not only reproduces life, but also gives it form,"[8] the author asserts, in the Plot which follows, that his intention is "mezclar natura con bemol" ("to mix nature with 'musical sweetness,' 'delight' ") (Dedication, 34);[9] that is, in agreement with the Renaissance ideal, to present the truth with entertainment, to soften artistically the scene of nature which he proposes to portray: "for that reason Lozana will come out much wiser in the story than she actually showed herself to be" (Plot, 36). So the author will also be able to teach while entertaining. From the beginning of the work, Delicado stands his ground on the fact that he writes it as much for the enjoyment of the "Illustrious señor," to whom the novel is dedicated, as for the pleasure of the readers, and for the amusement of those afflicted outcasts of Rome: "Thus I will administer forgetfulness for the pain" (Dedication, 34).

It should be noted, however, that the portrait was painted "also to bring to mind many things which occur in our times, which neither laud those present nor should serve as an example for those to come" (Dedication, 34). As Professor Hernández so well points out,[10] the author's intent is to search for the principal essence of his portrait within life's experience; to use veracity as a means and a goal of literary creation, presenting it artistically in order to entertain, and at the same time, to teach a moral lesson through the vision of human vanity, deception, the tragic life, and the sad end of many individuals. This technique was already very much in vogue in the classical theater of Aristophanes, who exposed his moral and didactic objectives with a comic wrapping, "clothing Justice in comic dress."[11] Consistent with classical tradition, therefore, the Dedication and the Plot, in monologue form, serve to familiarize the reader with the subject of the work and the circumstances of the action which will be developed in the various memoranda and elaborated, explained, and defended in the final pages.[12] In addition to presenting the author's artistic intention, the preliminary pages also affirm the didactic ends of the work.

Before beginning the narration of his protagonist's life, the author reminds us, in the beginning of Part One, that here "begins the story or portrait taken from the natural *jure cevil* ["civil law," "civil register"] of lady Lozana" (I, 37). With the civil register, interpreted here in the sense of nature, just as it is found in Rome, Delicado emphasizes his intention of basing his portrait on a real model, and not on something belonging to the world of fantasy. To maintain his intention of creating a work based on reality, the author projects his narration within the structural scheme of a portrait taken from the "civil register" of Rome, assuring his readers that he will give a faithful account of the actions of his heroine and of the world in which she lives; in the same way he aptly employs the *mamotreto* ("memorandum") and not the "chapter," as a means to attain his purpose. So he says, at the beginning of Part One, that this portrait "goes in memoranda because in such a work it is appropriate" (I, 37). *Lozana* is better adapted to memoranda, Delicado elaborates in his Explanation of the work, because this word means: " . . . a book which contains different thoughts and compilations joined together. Precisely because in similar secular works one can put neither name nor word which pertains to the books on good and holy doctrine, in this whole portrait there is not a single thing which addresses the religious nor the holy, nor has anything to do with the churches, ecclesiastics, or other things done which should not be said" (Explication, 250).

The pages of *Lozana* demonstrate, nevertheless, that nothing nor anyone escapes the reality of this portrait. Implicit in the protagonists' words there is much which can be deduced about false religiosity and the bad habits of clerics, one of whom leaves the pretty Cordovan girl pregnant (XXIII, 108). Thus in *Lozana*, "memorandum" does not replace "chapter" because it is a secular work in which "one should not put either name or word which pertain to books about good and holy doctrine." Rather, within the entire scope of the author, the division of the work into a series of memoranda can be justified in part by what he tells about the nature of *Lozana:* "a book which contains different thoughts" and also by the definition of the word *mamotreto* as found in the Dictionary of the Spanish Royal Academy: "The book or notebook which serves for jotting down the things which are needed to be kept at hand in order to be put in order later."[13] With regard to *mamotreto,* there exists, moreover, another possible justification for its use. Observe the relationship between the sensual content of the work and the double meaning of the word. In memorandum LXIII, Lozana explains to the woman pilgrim "that the woman without a man is like fire without firewood. And let the smart man light her up and eat a slice of bacon and in this way make *mamotretos* when his time comes" (p. 238).

As an element of structure, the memorandum, seen in terms of a notebook which serves for "jotting down" and "compiling" different things and thoughts, is particularly useful to Delicado who wants to gather the details of the portrait of a woman known to him and of a society dominated by vice and corruption. Concerning his desire to be exact and concise in his task of portrait painter, it is significant to note the following reference which Delicado makes on the technique of "taking note" not only of what he sees and hears, but also of what he remembers. In memorandum XLII the author tells Rampín: "Here, take this and bring me a little bit of paper and ink, for I want to make a note of something which I have just remembered" (p. 176). Thus, *Lozana* becomes a type of diary-novel in which each memorandum represents a part of the social register of Delicado's world.

The use of the diary as a literary instrument permits the material of the novel to be narrated and lived at the same time. Concurrently, this technique gives the reader a notable sensation of intimacy with the narration and, especially, with the narrator. The expediency of the memorandum, as a part of the total diary, also creates the impression of a logical chronology in the presentation of the novelistic facts and events.[14] This is well delineated in *Lozana,* where the protagonist's life and vicissitudes in Rome are projected against an historical background from 1513, when she witnesses the coronation of Leo X, until 1527, when she is a witness to the sack of Rome.

Within the artistic and moral objective of the author, the portrait he presents of this beautiful woman, daring and lusty, is well delineated, and in the sixty-six memoranda the protagonist is seen in the principal stages of her life — from her juvenile years, in the morally doubtful atmosphere of her parents and relatives (I - III), her encounter and her life with Diomedes, "her dear lover" (III - IV), the professions which she follows to earn her living in Rome, among them that of courtesan and go-between (V - LXV), up to her rejection of her licentious way of life (LXVI). The memorandum as part of a "diary" is thus an excellent means of achieving the author's goal of being faithful to the model in every detail which he narrates: "This portrait is so natural, that there is no person who knew Lozana, in Rome or outside of Rome, who will not recognize her clearly from her acts, activities and words; I have tried hard not to write a single thing the essence of which I did not first take from my model, looking into her or at her" (Plot, 36).

In the artistic scheme of *Lozana,* the first four memordanda form what has been called in the picaresque genre, the "prehistory" of the novel.[15] In these pages, the description of the protagonist as a woman of "intelligence and thorough knowledge, ... genius ... and great vivacity, ... beauty ... grace and boldness," offers us a logical antecedent to the fifth memorandum wherein is narrated "How [Lozana] succeeded in finding the way to live by using audacity instead of wisdom." A new level in the narration of the protagonist's life begins here. The important thing for the author now, in his effort to create a realistic portrait, is the analysis of Lozana's behavior and of her reaction to meeting a variety of people: her compatriots, mischievous laundresses, young rascals in search of masters, nobles — both rich and poor — canons living in concubinage, and every type of courtesan.

II *Dialogue*

In memorandum V, the reader begins to realize that the portrait which is being formed possesses an extraordinary vivacity, somewhat theatrical,[16] created by the lifelike dialogue which is here, and will be in all the following memoranda, the major vehicle of expression. The dialogue form of the two central parts of *Lozana* is indispensable to the author's purpose of painting with words his protagonist and the world around her, since only through dialogue can the author capture the characters' expressions and feelings, the spontaneity and intimacy of their actions.

Concerning this point, Alfonso Reyes affirms: "Delicado not only narrates but he also reproduces dialogues of the characters among themselves and dialogues between himself as the author and his characters."[17] In effect, the lively dialogue, written in the present tense, "gives the sensation that what is happening is something alive, something which is occurring right before our very eyes."[18] Note the following fragment of memorandum IX, in which Lozana, recently arrived in Rome, begins to seek information about the people there. This dialogue between Lozana and Beatriz demonstrates how Delicado creates this lifelike sensation of the world which he proposes to paint (IX, 55):

Lozana. Tell me, dear ladies, are there any Jews here?
Beatriz. Many, and they are our friends; if you should need something from them, they will do you courtesy and honor for the love of us.
Lozana. And do they deal with Christians?
Beatriz. Well, don't you notice them?
Lozana. And which ones are they?
Beatriz. Those who wear the red badge.
Lozana. And do the women wear a badge, too?
Beatriz. No, señora, they go throughout Rome preparing and adorning brides and selling refined calomel and waters for the face.
Lozana. I would like to see that.

Lozana. Decíme, señoras mías, ¿hay aquí judíos?
Beatriz. Munchos, y amigos nuestros; si hubiéredes menester algo d'ellos, por amor de nosotros os harán honra y cortesía.
Lozana. ¿Y tratan con los cristianos?
Beatriz. Pues ¿no los sentís?
Lozana. ¿Y cuáles son?
Beatriz. Aquéllos que llevan aquella señal colorada.
Lozana. ¿Y ellas llevan señal?
Beatriz. Señora, no; que van por Roma, adobando novias y vendiendo solimán labrado y aguas para la cara.
Lozana. Eso querría yo ver.

Lozana and the other characters of this literary portrait, as well as the artist who depicts them, reveal a strong desire for visual contact with things. We find references to the visual throughout the work: "And looking, I saw much better" (Author: Plot, 36); "Because of my desire to see him, I didn't worry about eating" (Lozana: VI, 48); "I want to go to see how she talks and what she buys" (Silvio: XXIV, 113); "This morning I saw there a lodging-house" (Squire: XXXIV,

147); "He is praised who looks, notes, and learns in time" (Lozana: XLVI, 185).

In the quoted dialogue between Lozana and Beatriz, the emphasis is on the auditory, plastic, and visual element. Through the use of the verb *sentís,* in the sense of "hear" "perceive" or "notice," the author invites the reader to imagine the noise of a large crowd of busy merchants. Among them were Jewish businessmen wearing the distinguishing red badge. Soon Lozana's eyes and ours focus on another group of people, women who specialize in the art of rejuvenation. The mention of calomel, a yellowish-white mercurial powder, and waters for the face, cosmetics which serve as a base for makeup, reinforces the importance which the theme of cosmetics has in *Lozana.* The frequency with which this topic appears in the work reflects the author's awareness of the things which are a part of life to such an extent that the cosmetics here, as in *Celestina,* become representative of "a type of plastic dialogue, a visual dialogue."[19]

By means of a visually expressive dialogue the author presents the sights of the city as well, the piazzas and streets through which Rampín and Lozana walk and the points of interest which they find there. In accordance with this purpose, the title of memorandum XII is, in part, "How Rampín shows [Lozana] the city . . .":

Rampín. . . . through this street you go to Campo de Flor and to the Colosseum, and right here is the bridge, and these fellows are the bankers.
Lozana. Oh, I would not want them to recognize me because I have always been on demand.
Rampín. Come this way and watch. Many things are sold here, and all the best found here in Rome and outside of Rome is brought here. . . . I can show you the bronze statue of Rodriguillo, the Spaniard, who is seen taking a thorn out of his feet and is naked. The statue was made in Campidolio.
Lozana. Upon my soul, that's something important to see and know! . . .
Rampín. Do you see over there the steam baths where the Romans came out?
Lozana. By your father's life, let's go there!

Rampín. . . . por aquí se va a Campo de Flor y al Coliseo, y acá es el puente, y éstos son los banqueros.
Lozana. ¡Ay, ay! No querría que me conociesen, porque siempre fui mirada.
Rampín. Vení por acá y mirá. Aquí se venden munchas cosas, y lo mejor que en Roma y fuera de Roma nace se trae aquí. . . . os puedo mostrar al Rodriguillo español de bronzo, hecha su estatua en Campidolio, que se saca una espina del pie y está desnudo.

Meaning and Form of Lozana [69]

Lozana. ¡Por mi vida, que es cosa de saber y ver! . . .
Rampín. ¿Veis allí la estufa dó salieron las romanas?
Lozana. ¡Por vida de tu padre, que vamos allá!

And later, in memorandum XV, there is described "How they wandered through Rome observing . . .":

Lozana. Which way should we go?
Rampín. This way, by the Plaza Redonda, and you'll see the Pantheon and the tomb of Lucretia, the virtuous Roman woman, and the stone obelisk in which are preserved the ashes of Romulus and Remus, and the carved column, a magnificent thing, and you'll see Setemzonéis. . . .
Lozana. What plaza is this?
Rampín. This is called Nagona. . . .

Lozana. ¿Por dó hemos de ir?
Rampín. Por aquí, por Plaza Redonda, y verés el templo de Panteón, y la sepultura de Lucrecia Romana, y el aguja de piedra que tiene la ceniza de Rómulo y Rémulo, y la colona labrada, cosa maravillosa, y veréis Setemzonéis. . . .
Lozana. ¿Qué plaza es ésta?
Rampín. Aquí se llama Nagona. . . .

The stimulating factor in these dialogues is Lozana's curiosity to know the city of Rome, the interest she has in seeing and knowing all that surrounds her. To travel and to see is to know: "The one who walks a lot knows more than the one who has lived a lot, because the one who lives a lot each day hears new things, and the one who gets around sees what will be heard" (L, 196). Lozana's desire "to know and to experience" (p. 107)[20] brings her to a dialogue with Rampín, who answers her with a brief, cursory, and sometimes graphic exposition of what they see and are going to see.

In *Lozana,* the dialogue is thus an artistic and an extremely effective means by which the author reproduces successfully an authentic portrait of the physical and historical reality of Renaissance Rome. Through the dialogue the Roman world becomes real in its totality: the majestic beauty of the monuments of imperial Rome, the enchantment of the modern districts and the tumult of the piazzas and markets are seen. Nevertheless, the dialogue in Delicado's work is not limited to giving us knowledge of the external world.

The Renaissance, says Ortega y Gasset, "uncovers in all its vast amplitude the internal world, the *me ipsum,* the conscience, the subjective,"[21] and Delicado, by means of the dialogue, provides a full report of human experiences: he reveals the behavior and the mentality and the way his personages act and think. The psychological character of the lozanesque world is magnificently perceived, for example, in the amorous scene of memorandum XIV, which describes "what happened between Lozana and her future servant in bed." The episode, which occupies virtually all of the memorandum, is too long to be reproduced here, so we shall simply analyze it by citing only the particularly relevant expressions and words. The interested reader is invited to consult the entire passage of the text. We will recall that after spending her first day with Rampín exploring the wonders of Rome, Lozana retires to bed where she is surprised by the young picaro. The ensuing conversation which passes between them is reproduced with total frankness and "with a naturalness of language absolutely unique in the Spanish novel."[22] Within *Lozana,* however, the scene is typical of the effective and vital form as it is of the *joie de vivre* of the whole work. With a series of exclamatory expressions and rhetorical questions the picture of the two protagonists, wrapped up in the mutual desire for pleasure, achieves a lively and dynamic movement. The interjection ¡*Ay!* ("Oh!") gives the impression of the young girl's sudden surprise and of the delight which accompanies the sexual satisfaction. The elliptical phrases in which are repeated variations of the verb *hacer* ("to do"), *hacéis* ("you do"), *haré* ("I will do"), *haréis* ("you will do"), *hará* ("it will do"), denote the emphasis on the rapid movement of the action. Alliterated, metaphorical and onomatopoeic words and expressions add to the already lively dialogue a plastic and visual expressive force. Here are some examples: *dinguilindón* ("bell clapper"; in jargon, "male organ"); *frenillo* ("frenum," "prepuce"); *copo y condedura* ("grabbing and everything else," "the caresses and copulation"); *coso* ("bull-ring"; in jargon, "vagina"); *garrocha,* ("spear"; "the picador's goad," "the male organ"); *a la machamartillo* ("to the tune of the hammer"); ¡*A las clines, corredor!* ("grab the mane, runner!" animating cheers so that the man will persevere in his action); ¡*Agora, por mi vida, que se va el recuero!* ("Now, the mule-driver goes, upon my life!" metaphorical allusion to orgasm).

In the presentation of the bedroom scene, the author successfully carries out his task of portrait-artist. He arranges with obvious ability the details of the artistic picture, employing words and images with great connotative force, and exploiting the properties of the language to give rhythm and movement to the scene. The rhyme which is created with *poquito* ("a little while") and *bonito* ("nice"), and the use of the diminutives *pasico* ("gently"), *bonico* ("pretty one"), and *quedico* ("easy"), create a euphonic sound which suggests a perfect sensation of the intimate reality of the two characters. Exclamations like ¡*Catá que me apretáis!* ("Watch out, you are squeezing me!"), ¡*por allí van allá*! ("This is the way it goes!"), ¡*Sus dalde,... enlodá!* ("Go to it, ... give all you've got!") ¡*Aguza, aguza, dale si le das!* ("Sharper," "hit it," "hit it again," "hurry up if you're going to do it!") contribute to the rapid rhythm of this scene and provide an emotionally ascending gradation which culminates with the final climax: ¡*Aquí, aquí, buena como la primera, que no le falta un pelo!* ("Here, here, a good one like the first; not a hair's difference!").

The apparently gay and unembarrassed tone of the bedroom scene pervades the whole work; and the dialogue, conceived as "the language which results from the meeting of two lives,"[23] is the vehicle with which the author achieves his goal of painting a natural portrait. To consider these expressions and words as no more than part of a pornographic scene is a grave error of critical judgement. Unfortunately, Henry Spencer Ashbee did interpret them in this way. Under the pseudonym of Pisanus Fraxi, he published some fragments of Delicado's work in his *Catena Librorum Tacendorum* (Bibliography of Forbidden Books), reproducing the entire dialogue between Lozana and Rampín.[24]

Delicado's intention, as I interpret it, was not to write pornographic literature, but to reproduce artistically what he saw occurring in his time. In other words, it is as important to look at the fragment alluded to above as it is to consider the entire work in its proper historical and social perspective, within the relaxed world of its times, in which there prevailed the spirit of sensuality and pleasure. The historical and literary documentation of Machiavelli,[25] Guicciardini,[26] Burckhardt,[27] and Graf,[28] offers many examples of the liberal thought and the concupiscent attitudes of Renaissance man; consequently, what is important in Delicado's work, what has real merit, is the author's unequaled ability to represent artistically not only the external world but also to capture, in a way no less realistic and vital, "the psyche,"[29] and the intimacy of his characters.

From the point of view of the artist who tries to paint with words the portrait of two individuals in the pursuit of pleasure, the primordial model exists in nature, in the world which surrounds him. The fact that the author does not want to reproduce in these pages an obscene picture of the model is indicated by his consciousness of the fundamental stylistic requirements of the work of art. In hiding the crude reality of the moment by linguistic and stylistic means (metaphorical expressions and words, onomatopoeic and funny expressions, as, for example, *lanza* ("spear"), *majadero ("fool") unicornio* ("unicorn") and *ese hurón no sabe cazar en esta floresta* ("that ferret doesn't know how to hunt in this forest"), Delicado diverts our attention from the sexual act toward the artistic expression of the same, which brings the reader to react not so much in an emotional way as in an aesthetic way. This technique is clearly explained by Edwin Hood who says that "the poet, . . . most exuberant and overflowing with just and admirable appreciation of delightful scenes, and thoughts, and impressions, will, by consequence, frequently overflow too with the contrastive affluence of words, moulding themselves into wit, of a mode of discourse admirably humoursome."[30]

Let us remember that in the creation of his portrait, Delicado's intention "was to mix nature with 'musical sweetness,' 'delight,' " that is, to portray nature with a charming tone of entertainment. Making use of this artistic sensibility, Delicado, instead of describing the model in a crude form which would excite the reader emotionally, succeeds in painting a scene with a splendid and humorous expression of delight.[31] It would be difficult not to enjoy this scene of Lozana and Rampín in which irony and humor abound. It is sufficient to think about the manner in which the astute Lozana, passionately awaiting her new — and old — experience with Rampín, hurries to tell him: "Look, I have a husband," and, a little later, "I want to tell you the truth, I am a virgin," culminating quickly with the full submission: "Here goes honor!" The effect which this scene produces is more comical than pornographic. The comicalness of this amorous affair can be related with what Burckhardt says about the technique used by the Renaissance novelists. These, the Swiss writer comments, give us to understand that love consists solely in sensual pleasure, "and that to win this, all means, tragic or comic, are not only permitted, but are interesting in proportion to their audacity and unscrupulousness."[32]

In other parts of *Lozana,* Delicado's linguistic audacity can be appreciated in the transposition of meaning of words associated with the domestic activity of women as, for example, *ordir* ("to prepare the warp"), *tramar* ("to weave"), *tejer* ("to knit") (I, 37); *hilar* ("to spin") (LVI, 217); *tela* ("cloth") (XXXIX, 165); *lino* ("flax") (LXI,

232) — words which become, in Delicado's work, metaphors for sexual activity and the material aspirations of Lozana. There is also to be found the transposition in the meaning of words associated with the religious as, for example, the *cirio pascual* ("Paschal candle") (XVII, 88), the candle which is blessed on Holy Saturday, interpreted in its double meaning, as the male organ; *ilesia y el campanario* ("the church and the belfry") which Rampín mentions when he suggests to Lozana the position he wants: *metamos la ilesia sobre el campanario* (". . . let's put the church on top of the belfry") (XIV, 77).

The antiphrases used in sensual contexts are deep-rooted in literary tradition. Manuel Criado de Val, in his study "Antífrasis y contaminaciones de sentido erótico en *La Lozana Andaluza*" (Antiphrases and Contaminations of Erotic Meaning in *Lozana*),[33] points out that the sources of this tradition are found in classical, Arab, Provençal, and Spanish celestinesque literature, all of which, it seems, Delicado must have known quite well. It must be noted, however, that Delicado, in order to achieve the erotic sense through the transposition of meaning of words, did not only make use of existent literary traditions, but also of his direct contact with the speech of the brothel, which, as Criado de Val affirms, "Delicado not only knew, but also observed with a 'philologist's attentiveness,' incredible for his time."[34]

There is thus reflected in the language of *Lozana* the spirit of those whom the author portrays, as for example, Lozana and Rampín, in the amorous scene, depicted with a blending of colors of singular wit and charm. With the bedroom episode the author revives the gay Roman life, and thus he entertains us, thinking, perhaps, of his protagonist's words: "If I wouldn't discuss this with anyone, it wouldn't be worth anything, not having been celebrated with the god of laughter" (LI, 198). The humorous intention of Delicado is underlined in the title of memorandum XLI: "Here the third part of the portrait begins, where there will be funnier things than in the past one" (p. 171). Nevertheless, as Lincoln Rothschild points out in his excellent study on the dynamism of art as a cultural expression, "the truly creative artist is a man of purposeful action,"[35] as is Delicado in the constructive plan of his work. This is confirmed by the fact that both the scene between Rampín and Lozana and the rest of the descriptions of the happy and libertine Roman life are sketched with a didactic goal which reminds us of Erasmus's teaching that "all enjoyment and amusement is only condiment of folly";[36] a lesson which

Delicado takes from his profound understanding of the world surrounding him, of the nature of man, of the fugacity of time, and of the brevity of human pleasures.

Certainly, by introducing a humorous element into the portrait, Delicado fulfills his desire to still the sad memories of the destruction of Rome, of which the poor refugee Spaniards, as well as he himself, were witnesses. But what is even more significant is his intention to project, beneath the funny and amusing narrations, the moral lesson, the real goal of his work; this is in accordance with the teaching of the classical Greeks and Latins, which Horace recapitulates when he asks: "What forbids telling the truth to one who is laughing? Teachers give sweets to children, so that the latter will be willing to start learning."[37] The linguistic artifices which color various passages of *Lozana* with a comic hue are the "sweets" which the author uses to coax the reader to learn the moral lesson.

III Satire

The humorous element has, thus, a notable importance for Delicado as a moralist who wants to present the didactic lesson, the teaching of the futility of man's anxieties and pleasures, with the "musical sweetness" of entertainment. It is also of particular usefulness to Delicado as a satirist. As Leonard Feinberg points out, one of the main aspects of the satirical writer is his talent of comic deformation to ridicule and criticize the world around him, that is, the affectations of individuals and the corruption of institutions.[38] Another critic, David Worcester, in his meritorious work on the art of satire, says that satirical writers, like the religious reformers, are interested in exposing the social abuses in order to arrive at a didactic goal.[39] However, in order to achieve effectively this ethical goal through the use of satire, the author needs to employ certain artistic means, because, "without style and literary form, his message would be incomprehensible; without wit and compression it would not be memorable. . . ."[40] The stylistic resources which Delicado employs in describing the scene between Rampín and Lozana are a manifest example of how the author realizes his desire of arriving at the moral lesson, laughing, with us, at human folly.

Delicado reinforces his didactic intention by presenting, at times, a satirical picture of the amoral world of Rome in which selfishness, dishonesty, presumption, and vanity are the norms of conduct for all: servants, courtiers, noblemen, and clergy. If in some parts he presents his satire with a comic wrapping, created by the use of words with a double meaning, onomatopoeia, and metaphors, in other cases the message is more direct and serious, as we see in the description of the perennial corruption of servants: "Look, the young porters and the servant girls are those who discredit the houses, for they always go around talking ill of their master and they always make away with more than they earn, and they always have a box outside of the house for what they steal" (XV, 82).

Such social details, artistically presented, are appreciated also in connection with the descriptions Delicado makes of the life and customs of the Roman courtesans, given to luxury, elegance and ostentation. There ingenious comparisons and similes abound. To the portrait of the libertinism and vanity of the courtesans and the selfish servants Delicado adds, with a particularly ironic tone, the image of the nobles' pretension, as is perceived in Lozana's exclamation upon seeing the poor nobleman Saracín: "By Jove, you are both a knight and a nobleman, although poor!" (LXIV, 239). These words remind us of the third part of *Lazarillo,* a work which bears a notable picaresque affinity with Delicado's novel in its literary realism and, to a certain extent, as Francisco Márquez Villanueva observes, in the social vision which it projects.[41]

In the artistic representation of the lozanesque world we also find the burlesque caricature of clerics. Lozana tells the lady shirtmaker: "And there was another lady grocer there ... who brought with her a friar, a Brother of the Order of Mercy who has a nose like a pitcher's handle and a foot like a galley's oar" (VII, 50). The technique of grotesque caricature which Delicado employs to deform the friar's figure complements well the ignoble image which he wants to paint of the sensuality, abuses, and ambitions of the clergy. In memorandum XXXV, Lozana asks the maid Jacomina not to awaken the courtesan because "the abbot didn't let her sleep all night" (p. 149), an apparently frequent clerical activity paid for by "the dispatching of papal bulls ... " (XXXIII, 145). However, the greatest sin committed by that corrupted clergy is not their abuses nor their libertine conduct but rather their excessive pride, splendidly portrayed in the following dialogue (XII, 62):

Lozana. Who is this? Is he the Bishop of Córdova?
Rampín. My father should live like that! He is an ill-fated bishop from Spigant.[42]
Lozana. A mameluke's[43] triumph is greater.
Rampín. The cardinals here are like mamelukes.

Lozana. Those have themselves adored.
Rampín. And so do these fellows.
Lozana. They certainly show a lot of pride.

In accordance with what Holy Scripture teaches us, that "pride goes before destruction, and a haughty spirit before a fall" (Pr. 16: 18), Rampín adds that "they will tell me about it in '27" (XII, 62), with an obvious allusion to the imminent destruction of Rome that will take place with the sack of 1527. If earlier, in the description of the bedroom episode between Lozana and Rampín and their passionate, but ultimately vain, pursuit of pleasure we were reminded of Erasmus's lesson on human folly, the vision of the presumptuous cleric here also brings to mind the Dutch reformer's thoughts on the proud man. In the *Handbook of the Christian Soldier,* Erasmus expresses his concern about the conduct of priests, and in the *Praise of Folly* he explicitly discusses the immorality of the abbots and the contemptuousness of clerics and theologians who consider themselves "somewhat more than men," "supermen."[44] In this he anticipates the view held by Juan Luis Vives that "The prideful desires nothing so much as some similarity with God."[45]

The similarity of *Lozana* to Erasmian writings has been mentioned by Serrano Poncela, who affirms that Delicado, "a good Christian in his own way, although neither extremely devout nor a hypocrite, shared points of contact with the Erasmian currents."[46] Nicasio Salvador Miguel underlines this point by maintaining that *Lozana* is related "to the literary world of ecclesiastical criticism of Erasmian origin, which was so much in vogue in the Renaissance."[47] This criticism was substantially directed against the abuses of an unworthy clergy which shirked their Christian responsibilities with respect to charity. Thus, the following words of Lozana do not surprise us: "I want to see two things in Rome before I die: one, that friends be friends in times of prosperity as well as in times of adversity, and the other, that charity be practiced rather than preached, for, as you can imagine, it is never seen, it is only written, painted, or heard" (LII, 199 - 200). In Renaissance Rome, charity exists in name only; both the clergy and the rest of the inhabitants are involved in their search for the immediate pleasure to such an extent that Rome becomes "a sinners' refuge" (XXIV, 120). In the eyes of the author, human vanity and the lack of charity justify the providential punishment of Rome we see so clearly represented in the Epilogue, to be discussed at the end of this chapter.

Meaning and Form of Lozana

In his treatment of the Roman courtesans Delicado arrives at the moral lesson through frequent references to the danger of syphilis, which constantly menaces them, and also by means of allusions to the futility and brevity of their vain ambitions. He also attains a didactic goal by satirically portraying the servants' selfishness, and the corruption and presumption of the nobles and clergy. At times, Gilbert Highet comments, satire "wounds and destroys individuals and groups in order to benefit society as a whole,"[48] and there is no doubt that Delicado, like various moralists of the epoch, criticized the social abuses precisely to foment the spiritual improvement of that Renaissance society which he portrays. In this respect he differs greatly from Juvenal, whom he purports to imitate. The classical writer draws vivid and drastic pictures of the worst sides of Roman life and social conditions of his day, "without, as a rule, appealing for or even suggesting reforms."[49]

In order to make the moral message inherent in his work more pleasant and acceptable, Delicado frequently introduces a humorous element, following the model of the Greek playwrights and of Horace, who, while discussing the ethical and social problems of his time, proposes also to tell the truth, laughing. This is evident in the way in which the author describes the above-mentioned scene between Rampín and Lozana, in the stylistic resources which he employs in order to capture humorously the eagerness for the momentary pleasure of the two protagonists. As a satirical writer, Delicado could fit in the group of those which have been called "optimists," for whom evil and folly are not innate diseases in human nature but rather mistakes which can be corrected.[50]

The satirical technique used to underscore the moral lesson strengthens itself in Delicado's work by the use of the literary portrait, an artistic device with which the author captures a reality of which he is an integral part. Highet comments that a satirical portrait of a particular world must appear to be a photographic representation, and, in fact, a caricature, of the vices, hypocrisies, and illusions of those who live in it, something which is "most successfully achieved by authors who are, or pretend to be, themselves, part of the ludicrous and despicable pattern of human life."[51] As we have seen, Delicado is actually one of the protagonists of his novel, a character who could be called witness-narrator.[52] Delicado lives and acts in the world of his work, and he participates with his characters in the search for pleasures, and, like his protagonist, he experiences disenchantment with worldly pursuits.

Leonard Feinberg rightfully suggests that "the satirist's critical attitude has usually been explained on the grounds of his disillusionment,"[53] and in no part of *Lozana* does the author manifest better this disillusionment with human vanity than in his entreaty to the Lord, at the end of his work: "Turn away my eyes, Lord, that they may not see vanity" (LXVI, 246). Our author, like the characters of his work, has lived and sinned in the world which surrounds him; he has arrived at a realization of the futility of worldly things and now he wants to flee vanity, something which represents in the novelistic genre "an education into the realities of the material world and of human life in society."[54]

IV Style

If Delicado is successful in artistically reproducing the Renaissance Roman world and the sentiments of those who live in it, by means of a coherent structure and revealing dialogue, he is successful also on account of the stylistic variety with which he creates his work. In this study, style, dialogue, and structure are considered in their totality, as part of the Aristotelian concept of form; nevertheless, the distinction which Huntington Brown makes between the form, the larger aspects of a work of art, "its principal ... outlines"[55] (external elements of structure), and the details or the style of the same work is pertinent here. For him, this distinction corresponds precisely to that between "cut" and "weave" in the art of the tailor. Following this analogy between the "weave" and the style, we can penetrate deeper into an examination of the stylistic "weave" of *Lozana,* in order to point out, even more, its linguistic heterogeneity.

Delicado's literary portrait is taken from historical reality, and, consequently, we find in it the representation of a great variety of persons living in the Eternal City at the beginning of the sixteenth century (Italians, Catalans, Castilians, Jews, and converts), with a wide representation of professions and social positions (clergy, noblemen, servants, shirtmakers, prostitutes, and dentists). This conglomeration of individuals and of social classes is reflected, logically, in the manner in which the author reproduces their speech in the pages of his work. The majority of the more than 125 characters of *Lozana* have assimilated Italian so well that the use of Italian phrases, words, and Italianisms is nearly universal. During her time in Rome, Lozana herself achieves a notable proficiency in Italian, as can be noted in the passage in which she instructs the young Coridón in the method of attaining the woman he desires (LV, 214 - 215):

Lozana. ¡Ay, amarga, no ansí! Y tanto ceceas; lengua d'estropajo tienes. Entendamos en lo que dirás a tu amiga cuando esté sola, y dilo en italiano que te entienda: "Eco, madona, el tuo caro amatore; se tu voi yo mora soy contento. Eco colui que con perfeta fede, con lacrime, pene y estenti te ha sempre amato e tenuta esculpita in suo core. Yo soy Coridone, tuo primo servitore. ¡Oh mi cara Polidora, fame el corpo felice, y serò sempre tuo, Jaqueta, dicta Beatrice! Y así podrás hacer tu voluntad.

Lozana. Oh, No! Not that way! And you lisp so much; you have the tongue of a dish-clout. Let us understand what you will say to your girlfriend when she is alone, and say it in Italian, so she'll understand you: "Here, my lady, is your dear lover; if you want me to die, I am happy. Here is the one who with perfect faith, with tears, pain and need has always loved you and kept you engraved in his heart. I am Coridone, your first servant. Oh my dear Polidora, make my body happy, and I will always be yours, Jaqueta, called Beatrice!" And in that way you can do whatever you want.

In his book Delicado tells us that the language of his characters is a living reflection of the speech in the world which surrounds him, and, therefore, he justifies reproducing words and phrases in Italian: "And if they ask why I put some words in Italian, I could do it writing in Italy" (Apology, 248). Torres Naharro had already incorporated exotic words in some scenes of his plays *Soldadesca* and *Tinelaria,* with the difference that for him this interest in including Italian words in his works "was a passing fancy born in an occasion and place in which his plays were performed for a principally Italian audience. On the contrary, the low and mongrel jargon in which *Lozana* is written is constant and systematic, like a transcript of what the author heard in the streets."[56] In effect, the author says that in producing this portrait, "I adjusted my writing to the sound in my ears" (Apology, 248).

Doubtlessly, what the author heard in the streets of Rome was a colloquial language full of words and phrases of the Italo-Hispanic populace, a language in which there abound neologisms, slang words, roguish jargon, proverbs, and familiar phrases. In the above-cited passage in which Lozana gives advice to Coridón we find some features of the popular speech: the interjection ¡*Ay, amarga!* ("Oh bitter!" "Oh no!"), the familiar expression *lengua d'estropajo* ("tongue of a dish-clout," for a lazy tongue which does not pronounce well), the use of the adverb *Eco* (modern Italian *ecco,* "here is"), and the frequency of the conjunction *y* ("and").

Besides its linguistic interest this passage is also important to underscore a primordial concept of *Lozana*: the eagerness for pleasure.

Lozana's discourse embraces two opposite poles of love: the noble one, "Here is the one who with perfect faith, with tears, suffering, and need, has always loved you and kept you engraved in his heart," and the vulgar one: "Oh, my dear Polidora, make my body happy...!" Lozana begins with a parody of courtly love, the essence of which is the suffering ("if you want me to die, I am happy," "tears," "pain"), and the spiritual desire ("heart"), and she finishes by advocating the fulfillment of sexual love, that "the body be made happy." This is the plan proposed by Lozana for the young Coridón to bring about his desire to "enjoy" the one he loves. The fact that the interest in making "the body happy" follows immediately after the reference to the lover as a "servant," devout and suffering, reflects a satirical and burlesque attitude toward that concept of love which insists on the progressive conquest of woman, on the preliminaries of love, and on the spiritual enjoyment of woman. The rejection of such a concept of love is manifested by the ease with which Lozana lets herself be seduced by Rampín in the already discussed memorandum XIV and in his cynicism when he learns that she has a husband: "Well, he's not here now to see us."

Lozana's discussion with the young Coridón demonstrates that such concepts of love as the courtly, the neoplatonic, and the Ovidian are out of place in Delicado's work. Lozana, in mixing the interests of the "heart" with those of the "body," ridicules those refined social traditions and makes them a vehicle for achieving the immediate pleasure: "And in that way you can do whatever you want." This burlesque parody of the idealized social refinement of courtly love is also noticeable in the dialogue between Lozana and her lover Diomedes, in the beginning of the work (III, 41 - 42):

Diomedes. Oh, Oh! What a wound! Because of you some servant of yours has pierced me in the heart with a golden arrow of love.
Lozana. You should not be surprised, Your Grace, for when you called me to come down, it seems to me that I saw a young boy, with a piece of cloth around his forehead, and he shot at me with something, I don't know what. It touched me on the left breast.

Diomedes. ¡Ay, ay!, ¡qué herida! Que de vuestra parte cualque vuestro servidor me ha dado en el corazón con una saeta dorada de amor.
Lozana. No se maraville vuestra merced, que cuando me llamó que viniese abajo, me parece que vi un mochacho, atado un paño por la frente, y me tiró no sé con qué. En la teta izquierda me tocó.

Meaning and Form of Lozana [81]

Lozana's answer reinforces the satirical view which the young woman has toward the language and the love concepts of the sentimental novel and the books of chivalry. This reaction against the lofty and at times metaphorical language of courtly love can be related to the author's aversion to intricate and obscure language in general. In memorandum XXIV, the author-character scolds the companion for his cryptic description of Lozana: "Tell me who she is and don't beat around the bush with roundabout expressions, but 'speak to me frankly, in the manner of the honeycake-maker' " (XXIV, 114). The author's demand complements his belief, expressed earlier in this chapter, that simplicity of style is his own best vehicle for the representation of reality: "I did not compose here in the style of fancy speech, nor did I take material from other books, nor did I steal eloquence, because little eloquence is enough to tell the truth" (Plot, 35).

In memorandum LIX we find again an example of Italian, this time in the dialogue between Lozana and Clarina. Upon insisting that the young woman from Cordova give her oil for her eyes, and upon realizing that the oil has already been promised to another courtesan, Clarina says (p. 227):

No te curar, Lozana, que non vollo que lei sea da tanto que abia questo, que yo te daró olio de ducenti ani, que me donó a mí micer incornato mio, trovato sota terra.

Don't worry, Lozana; I don't want her to have such importance as to have this; I will give you an oil that is two hundred years old, that my obstinate husband who is now dead gave to me.

The Italian which Delicado reproduces here, as in other passages, is contaminated logically by Spanish, and vice versa. Thus, the Italian *non ti curare* becomes *no te curar* ("don't worry"). The transformation of *non ti* to *no te*, the apocope of the *e* in *curare*, the phonetic reproduction of *vollo*, and the degemination of the consonants to give us *abia* and *ani* (instead of *abbia* and *anni*) all reflect the Spanish influence.

The two passages in Italian which we have seen up to now are the most complete of *Lozana*, although there are various other examples of Italian phrases and of Italianisms which fill the pages of the work, as, for example, *quanto voi de tuti* ("how much do you want for all these") (XXXI, 139); *tu ne mente per la cana de la gola* ("you lie unashamedly") (XXXI, 139); *fillolo, no, mas sempre ho voluto ben a spañoli* ("No, son, but I have always loved the Spaniards") (LVI, 216); *guadaño* ("earnings") (XI, 58); *mancha* ("tip") (XIII, 71); *cualque* ("some") (V, 46); *dubitaban* ("they were doubting") (LIII, 204); *acordo* ("agreement") (LXII, 234).

The use of Italian is noted also in the conjugation of the verb *estar* ("to be") with the auxiliary *ser* ("to be"): *es estada mundaria toda su vida* ("she has been worldly all her life") (VI, 48); in the use of the future indicative after *cuando* ("when"): *¿qué hará de sus pares ella cuando parirá?* ("what will she do with her placenta when she will give birth?") (XXIV, 116); and in the indefinite construction of the partitive *de los, de la* ("some"): *No curéis, que mi tía tiene gallina y nos dará de los huevos* ("Don't worry, my aunt has a hen and she will give us some eggs") (XIV, 77) and *Señor, comed de la salvia con vuestra amiga* ("Sir, eat some sage with your lady friend") (XLII, 117). As we can ascertain from the works of Terlingen,[57] Keniston,[58] and Beberfall,[59] the influence of Italian in *Lozana* is notable, and the abundance of Italian expressions and of Italianisms complements the author's intention of creating a realistic picture of the sixteenth-century Roman environment.

Although Italian and Italianisms predominate among the exotic words of *Lozana*, there also appear features of other languages, amalgamated in the popular speech of Rome. The variety of words includes Latinisms, Latin words and expressions, as, for example, *de nobis* ("of ours") (VII, 51); *cliéntulo* ("customer," "parishioner") (XLIII, 179); *vita dulcedo* ("life and sweetness") (XLIX, 195); *de quis vel qui* ("whosoever," "whichever") (LIV, 209); *Petrus in cunctis* ("Peter in all, in everything") (LVI, 216); *de singulis* ("of the rest," "successively") (LXII, 235); *penitus* ("absolutely," "entirely") (LXII, 236).

It is also interesting to observe the combination of Portuguese and Castilian in memorandum XXVII (p. 126):

> Las otras (as vossas) beso.
> Lozana. Y yo las suyas, una y boa (una [vez] y buena).
> Portugués. Señora, sí. Rapá (Robad) la gracia de Deus, so vuestro!

> I kiss your hands.
> Lozana. And I kiss yours, once and well.
> Portuguese. Yes, lady. By God's grace, I am yours!

Another example worthy of our attention is found in the dialogue, almost totally in Catalan, between the young Aguilaret (Aguilarico),

Meaning and Form of Lozana   [83]

his mother, the Segorbesa (Segorbian), the barber, Mossén Sorolla (Señor Sorolla). Here is a fragment of it (X, 56 - 57):

Sorolla. Ven ací, mon cosín Aguilaret. Veniu ací, mon fill. On seu estat? que ton pare t'en demana.
Aguilaret. Non vul venir, que vaich con aquesta dona.
Sorolla. Ma comare! Feu-vos ací, vereu vostron fill.
Segorbesa. Vens ací, tacañet.
Aguilaret. Qué voleu ma mare?, ara ving.
Segorbesa. Not cures, penjat, traidoret! Aquexa dona, hon te ha tengut tot vuy?

Sorolla. Come here, my cousin Aguilaret. Come here my son. Where have you been? Your father has been looking for you.
Aguilaret. I don't want to go, because I'm going with that lady.
Sorolla. Godmother! Come near, here you will see your son.
Segorbian. Come here, you miser.
Aguilaret. What do you want, mother? I'm coming right now.
Segorbian. There is just no help for you, is there, you scoundrel and traitor! Where did that lady keep you all day?

As we have seen, Delicado's heterogeneous world is reproduced with a corresponding variety of linguistic expressions, an integral stylistic aspect which adds veracity and vitality to the work. It was correctly observed that *Lozana* "far from being written in 'very lucid Castilian' as the frontispiece announces, is written rather in that *lingua franca* of Italo-Hispanic jargon used in Rome by the Spaniards of the lowest classes who had been residing there a long time, and who, without really having learned the foreign language, muddled their own language with all types of Italianisms. . . ."[60] And not only Italianisms, but also Latin, Portuguese and Catalan words and expressions.

This mixture of language which Delicado reproduces in his work adds a certain verisimilitude to the world which he portrays, as do the numerous familiar and proverbial phrases (about 150 of them) and the words and twists of slang. The characters of *Lozana*, at times incapable of finding an efficient way to express their feelings, make use of proverbs because, as Valdés tells Coriolano, in the *Dialogue of the Language*, "one of those ancient examples has more authority than any one I could make up."[61]

In her daily life, Lozana and the characters which surround her use "more proverbs than a book,"[62] as Sancho Panza says, since they reflect the acquired wisdom of long experience. The following are some of the adages and proverbs from Delicado's book: "As welcome as water in May" (Lozana: XIX, 100); "A donkey that carries you is worth more than a horse that makes you fall" (Imperia: LXII, 235); "Misery loves company" (Rampín: XII, 63); "I offer you Time as my witness" (The Neapolitan woman: XI, 59); "The sin which is kept a secret is half pardoned" (Camillus: XXXVIII, 162).[63]

As for the jargon, the vocabulary and the twists of slang, which, doubtless, the characters of the lozanesque world knew and understood quite well, the following examples give an idea of their tone: ¿*Salistes, chichirimbache*? ("Did you come out, coxcomb?") (XXIII, 142), where *chichirimbache* is a probable variant of *chiquiribaile*, meaning "coxcomb," "meddlesome man," "one who is clamorous and useless"; *"fue un emperador que, como viese que las mujeres tenían antiguamente cobertera en el ojo de cucharita de plata . . ."* ("there was in ancient times an emperor who, seeing that women had a silver teaspoon on the 'eye' as a cover . . .") (LXIII, 237), in which *ojo* ("eye") stands figuratively for the female genital part; *Tené punto, señora, que con ésta serán ocho . . ."* ("Be advised, lady, that there will be eight with this one . . .") (XX, 102), the verbal locution *tené punto,* with the meaning of "pay attention," "be advised."[64]

The linguistic richness of *Lozana* is indeed extraordinary. The many slang words, now rare and strange, formed in Delicado's epoch an integral part of the familiar language used by those with whom the author shared his life during various years in Rome. As a whole, the dialogue, the mixture of languages, the multitude of proverbs, slang words and expressions, create in *Lozana* a conversational style which reminds us of the statement which Valdés makes to Marcio in the *Dialogue of the Language*: "To tell you the truth . . . the style which I have is natural to me; without affectation, I write as I speak."[65] It is precisely this "spoken" language which gives life and veracity to Delicado's portrait. Menéndez Pelayo observed that "The language of *Lozana* is as unique as its plot and style,"[66] and we see also in this uniqueness the indisputable artistic consciousness of the author.

V *Apology*

This artistic awareness of Delicado can be perceived, furthermore, in the way in which the final parts of *Lozana* (Apology, Explanation, Epilogue, Letter of excommunication, Epistle, and Digression) fit within the total scheme of the work. The characterization of Lozána in the Dedication, as a person "with admirable ingenuity and clever art, great diligence, ... and conscientiousness" (p. 37), is enriched in the Apology, where the author praises her as "a very audacious woman" (p. 248). The author distinguishes her from all the other famous women of the portrait, for her "goodness, reputation, charity, continence, and faithfulness" (p. 247). In addition, the moral lesson related to human foibles, which the author himself projects in his work and which Lozana expresses quite well in her dialogue with Divicia, "I want to know and see and prove ... and in the end I found it was all vanity" (p. 207), is reinforced in the Apology. There the author extols Lozana for her wisdom in recognizing, in time, the futility of human strife and for seeking a life of peace on the island of Lipari.

More importantly, however, the Apology serves to reflect another significant aspect of Delicado's moral message, one that is particularly characteristic of Renaissance thought. The point in question stems from the author's laudatory comment on Lozana as a woman who "tried hard to avoid doing those things which were offensive to God or to His commandments" (p. 248). The validity of Delicado's judgment of his protagonist becomes plausible if we consider that he judges Lozana's conduct according to the Renaissance belief in the individuality of man and his tendency toward subjectivity even in the interpretation of religion. Jacob Burckhardt, in his study on the religious spirit of the Renaissance, asserts that although the representative individuals of that epoch were quite capable of distinguishing between good and evil, they were not conscious of sin.[67] Thus, in her life as a courtesan Lozana often talks laudably of the ability and the skill with which she uses the necessary means to be successful in that profession. For her and for the other individuals living in the lozanesque world, physical beauty and natural talents are seen as gifts of God's grace, as gifts of nature.[68] At the beginning of the novel the author tells us that it seemed to the young Lozana "that nature had reserved nothing for itself which it had not invested in her dear lover" (IV, 43). And, later, talking about a famous courtesan, Rampín declares, "Raise your eyes and you'll see God's creation in lady Clarina" (XII, 63). Clearly, therefore, these physical and intellectual attributes are considered good, and, as long as one does not do harm to his neighbor, he can enjoy them fully without preoccupation or blame.

After all, the author affirms, "It is a true saying which I have read many times, that 'whatever men do, the intention saves all' " (XLII, 178). Lozana's intention has been to survive in a new environment, to gain fame in her profession, and to help others: "With my reputation and ability I tried to offer some good words, to calm anger, to reconcile parties, to make peace, and to take away rancor" (XXXIX, 166). She does not admit remorse for her actions: "I can go anywhere unashamed, for I never committed any vile act, nor did I bring bawdy messages to vile persons, nor did I do any evil to gentlemen or respectable prostitutes" (XXXIX, 166).

Because of Lozana's view of life and of her sense of freedom from guilt in the religious sense, her "conversion," which is described in memorandum LXVI, and to which the author alludes in the Apology, is not owing to the idea of sin but rather to the realization of human vanity and pride; the abuses and the foolishness of man are the real causes of evil. She becomes weary of the human condition and for this reason she abandons her profession, leaves Rome and, "as does Peace, . . . she flees to the islands" (LXVI, 243).

Lozana's life trajectory, from her childhood in Spain to the years spent in Italy where she experiences life and becomes skillful in wordly things, to be later disillusioned, represents the essence of the novel as a literary genre. In the words of Maurice Shroder, the novel "records the passage from a state of innocence to a state of experience, from that ignorance which is bliss to a mature recognition of the actual way of the world."[69] Ortega y Gasset comments that "the myth (in the sense of complete transformation of reality through imaginative projection) is always the point of departure of all poetry, including realistic poetry. In this, however, we accompany the myth in its descent, in its fall. The theme of realistic poetry is the gradual destruction of an ideal."[70] Similarly, we could say that in the development of a novel like *Lozana* there exists a "demythification," that is, in Shroder's opinion "the formal or generic equivalent to the experimental disillusionment of the novel's protagonist."[71] The final disillusionment comes to Lozana when she completes the process of instruction in the realities of the material world and of human life: " . . . I wanted to know and see and experience as did Apuleius, and in the end . . . I harvested little fruit, and so do all those women who get lost in similar fantasies" (LIV, 207).

VI *Explanation*

The interdependence of the structural elements of *Lozana* is reflected in the declaration which the author makes in the Apology, where he explains that to understand the intention of his portrait it is necessary to read the preliminary pages; "and if someone should like to know from the author what his intention was in portraying Lozana and her followers reprovingly, let him read the beginning of the portrait" (p. 248). To appreciate the real meaning of the work and to understand the author's purpose, it is necessary to know it well, as we are told in the Explanation: "to enjoy this portrait and before gossiping about the author, people ought first to read it and understand it well" (pp. 250 - 51).

If the Apology brings more details about Lozana's personality to light, so does the Explanation. In the first memorandum the author enumerates the outstanding aspects of Lozana's personality, her impetuosity, vigor, exuberance, and intelligence: " . . . she [Lozana] was so keen that her mother almost did not need a business agent" (I, 37). Later, in memorandum XXXVI, the ambassador declares to the knight: "Lozana seems to me to be astute, for she certainly has something of the serpent and something of the dove" (p. 155). It was said of the dove that "there is no bird wiser nor more political . . . it's the one that knows best how to live . . . and the serpents are considered masters of all sagacity."[72] Thus, the ambassador's characterization of Lozana reinforces the description of her given by the author at the beginning of the work. Her characterization finds a logical conclusion in the pages of the Explanation, where the author again describes Lozana's beauty and exuberance (p. 250).

The Explanation has, in addition, the implicit function of underscoring the relation which exists in the work between its sometimes risqué material and its didactic intention. The author realizes that not all who read his book will be capable of harvesting the worthwhile fruit and, therefore, he underlines the importance of seeing the portrait in its totality: "if they look at it, what is lacking in the beginning will be found in the end" (Plot, 36). This realization that the material of the portrait can lead those who may not understand its real meaning to a bad interpretation, induces the author to assert, in the Explanation, that young children should not read it (p. 251).

VII *Epilogue*

The Epilogue is also significantly related to the rest of the work in general, and to the Dedication, in particular. As we have previously seen, Delicado dedicates his work to the "Illustrious señor," whose identity remains unknown in the beginning. Following the traditional norms, the author dedicates his work to a patron in the hope of receiving from him the necessary support for the success of his publication. Since it is a matter of a literary portrait, Delicado appropriately asks the "Illustrious señor" to "varnish" the portrait, in the metaphorical sense of giving prestige: "and as every portrait needs varnish, I beseech your lordship to give it, favoring my desire, and commending to discreet readers the pleasure and enjoyment which will come to them from reading about lady Lozana" (Dedication, 34). Among those who are going to enjoy the narration is the "Illustrious señor" himself, a man of "virtuous countenance," who "takes pleasure when he hears about matters of love ... and principally when he hears talk about people who are cognizant of those things pertaining to it" (Dedication, 33). These are the only references which Delicado makes to his patron until the Epilogue. There, a series of historical allusions recently studied by Giovanni Allegra reveal that the "Illustrious señor" is the prince who succeeded Hugh of Bourbon as commander of the Imperial forces which sacked Rome, Philibert of Chalôns.[73]

The discovery of the identity of Delicado's patron has shed new light on the author's popularity among his contemporaries, and particularly with the prince. Such popularity could have been achieved by Delicado for his publication of the treatise *On Consoling the Infirm*, dealing with the remedies of venereal disease. The prince, especially, would have wanted to know the Spanish writer at a time when his armies were being decimated by syphilis. As a result of his probable association with the renowned commander of the Imperial forces, Delicado sought him as his patron. The prince, familiar with the libertine Roman life and a witness to the city's destruction, would have the power to corroborate the authenticity of *Lozana*. He would also be able to strengthen the belief expressed in the novel that Rome was the recipient of a just punishment, a view held by both those who sacked the city and by Erasmian followers. On this point the Epilogue is clear: "Oh, you who will come after the punished, look at this portrait of Rome, and let no one be the cause of another like it. Look well at the portrait and at its end, which is the punishment of heaven and earth" (p. 253). The punishment (chaos, pestilence, and death), is graphically described in the Epilogue and in the Digression. Together the Epilogue and the Digression complete the work by supplying a logical conclusion to the several moral prophecies, scattered in the various memoranda, concerning the imminent destruction of the city. The Epilogue and the Digression also reinforce the principle expressed by the author: "You cannot flee Divine Providence" (p. 253). The author concludes the Epilogue with a reference to the artistic and moral objective of his portrait: ". . . because I composed it . . . to give solace and pleasure to readers and listeners, may they not look at my poor art but rather at my honest intention" (p. 254).

VIII *Letter of Excommunication*

The Letter of excommunication which follows the Epilogue is also a part which is significantly related to the rest of the work. This letter is a public condemnation of a woman known to Delicado, a woman who was the source of his past amorous passion and the cause of his present physical suffering, which was produced by syphilis. The severity of the denunciation reflects the pains which Delicado had to endure for many years of his life. The importance of the Letter is that it emphasizes the moral meaning of the work by showing that the author, like the characters in his portrait, suffers because of his licentious conduct. In fact, the common denominator of all those who live in Lozana's world is the eagerness for pleasure, the search for love deprived of every meaning in a world dominated by vice and corruption; and all of this in the center of Christendom! To the very end of the work, the life of the author remains intimately associated with the life of his protagonists.

IX *Epistle*

The Epistle is written by Lozana to her putative sisters in love: the courtesans of Rome and those women who intend to embrace the life of pleasure. The object of the Epistle is to show the futility of their efforts by pointing to the destructive results of the sack of Rome: ". . . fourteen thousand Teutonic barbarians entered, punished, and tortured us . . . and plundered . . ." (p. 257). Lozana's dramatic and vivid account of the event is followed by a nostalgic recollection of the glorious days past.

X *Digression*

The last part of *Lozana* is the Digression written by Delicado in Venice. In it he reiterates, as we have mentioned above, his views on the destruction of Rome as a just punishment for its social corruption. His views on Rome's fate have a distinct resemblance to those expressed by Alfonso de Valdés who saw in the sack of the Eternal

City "the effects of Divine fury."⁷⁴ Furthermore, Delicado reveals his necessity for sending *Lozana* to the printer, and the subsequent successful reception of the novel. He concludes by expressing hope that the work may truly be an instructive portrait to future generations.

XI Conclusion

In conclusion, *Lozana* is a work of art in which the formal elements complement, in an outstanding way, the artistic intention and the moral purpose of the work. *Lozana's* structural components, the functional and symbolic value of the preliminary pages, and of the dialogue, memoranda, and epilogues, satisfy fully the artistic exigencies of the classical authorities, such as Aristotle and Plato, according to whom the artist's effort ought to be directed toward giving definite and effective form to his work.⁷⁵ The Renaissance artist insists upon giving unity, harmony, and coherence, or better, a "legitimate construction,"⁷⁶ to the work of art. Delicado does not fail in this obligation. We can see his commitment to the artistic principles of the time in the well-developed and meaningful life trajectory of the protagonist and in the way in which the parts of *Lozana* are bound together.

The most widely used means of expression in *Lozana* is the dialogue through which we are shown a complete and concrete view of the Roman world. Vivid notes and references to the neighborhoods, streets, individuals, and their professions abound throughout the literary portrait, and they evoke an image of the entire city. In accordance with the author's intention of creating a "natural" portrait, our knowledge of the protagonist and of the other characters in the work, as in life, comes principally from their own words and actions. The spontaneity of the dialogues and the naturalness of style make *Lozana* a vibrating portrait of Renaissance Rome, a truthful portrait which serves as a vehicle for the exposition of the moral lesson. In his study on realism, John Laird observes that "Art, because it is representative, may be a vehicle of knowledge."⁷⁷ Indeed, through his portrait of the corrupt and vicious world of Rome, Delicado shows the futility of human aspirations and activities and the absurdity of those who blindly seek the "tree of folly."

"It was the work of the Renaissance . . . to awaken in man consciousness of his powers and to give him confidence in himself, to show him the beauty of the world and the joy of life."⁷⁸ Such spirit of the Renaissance touches Lozana; for this she takes pride in asserting her dignity and merit and her right to use the physical and intellectual attributes in full to enjoy what the world has to offer. The concomitant effect of this attribute is the formation of a strong individualism and a notable social amorality. Although this amorality existed without any sense of guilt, in the ethical sense of the word, it created, nevertheless, a milieu for the inevitable disenchantment man felt with worldly things.

CHAPTER 7

Picaresque Characteristics of Lozana

IN the literary tradition of Spain *Lozana* is one of the most notable antecedents of the picaresque novel,[1] which begins with the publication of the anonymous *Lazarillo de Tormes* (1554). As we mentioned in chapter 2, *Lozana* has been considered an important work of transition between *Celestina* and the picaresque novel.[2] It has also been seen by some critics as a literary creation that is close to being a picaresque novel[3] and by others as actually being the first picaresque novel.[4] Indeed, if we accept Professor Gilman's assertion that "Historically the *Lazarillo* lies in the immediate tradition of *Celestina*,"[5] of which *Lozana* is an obvious imitation, the relation of Delicado's work to the picaresque novel in general becomes very plausible.[6]

I *Background, Attributes, and Philosophy of the Protagonist*

In a way similar to the narration found in the "prehistory"[7] of the picaresque novel, Delicado begins his work with a description of the lowly origins and disreputable social environment of the protagonist. Lozana's father is a gambler and a pimp and her mother is a woman of dubious conduct. As in the case of the picaro, Lozana is seen as the product of her disreputable environment and upbringing. From her parents Lozana acquires a worldly education and licentious skills. Upon their death, she goes to live with an aunt, a woman of questionable character, who, seeing the girl's beauty and promiscuous inclinations, tells her, "Your physical attributes and your knowledge will be your dowry" (II, 39). Lozana's education in the sensual arts continues under the guidance of the aunt with whose shrewd advice she succeeds in captivating the wealthy merchant Diomedes, thereby securing, at least temporarily, a happy and carefree life.

The course of Lozana's life is also very similar to that of the picaro. The essence of both is the description of how the youth who is born or plunged into a dishonorable environment leaves home, struggles in a life of vagabondage, and reaches maturity with some form of social success. Lozana, like Lazarillo, is propelled into the world of picaresque vicissitudes with the confidence that she will succeed in life. Her aunt's words, "My child, be good, that fortune will be with you" (I, 38), are echoed in the edifying advice that Lazarillo's mother gives him as he embarks on the service of his first master. After leaving the aunt's house with Diomedes, Lozana begins a long journey that takes her to several parts of Europe, including northern Italy. The journey is itself a requisite of the picaresque narrative, as Pedro Penzol and Oldřich Bělič have shown.[8] We will recall that the happy interlude with Diomedes ends when his father, scornful of the Andalusian girl's relationship with Diomedes, has her stripped of all her possessions and arranges to have her taken to sea by a boatman with the intention of having her drowned. Probably impressed by her beauty and moved by pity, however, the boatman, instead of carrying out his assigned mission, takes Lozana to the safe port of Leghorn, and even gives her clothing. With a ring which Diomedes had given her, and which she had wisely hidden in her mouth, Lozana is able to buy a passage to the vicinity of Rome, thereby removing herself even more from the danger of the wrathful father.

The episode dealing with Diomedes' father is an eye-opener for Lozana, who comes to realize the harshness and deception of life and the need for ingenuity. As a result of that and subsequent episodes, Lozana, in the true spirit of the picaresque character, acquires a view of life as an adventure, as an experience from which she learns the key to survival and success. "He is praised who looks, notes, and learns in time," says Lozana, and she adds, "In my youth I wandered through the East, I went to Nigroponte, I saw and heard many things; at that time I observed, and now I benefit from what I watched then" (XLVI, 185).

Lozana's ingenuity and sagacity, described by Delicado at the beginning of the work, is revealed in all that she does and says. Note, for example, the tone of her words as she ponders on the state of her new life in Rome: "I know a great deal; if I now don't see to it that everyone becomes aware of my knowledge, it will all be for nothing" (V, 45 - 46). Such philosophy and her self-esteem incite Lozana to make her natural talents known and to enter into a variety of social circles. Like the picaros, Lozana begins her vicissitudes by skillfully performing various services, as we have seen, first as an expert in the art of cosmetics, then as a courtesan, and later as a go-between. With each change of profession Lozana rises in fame and in social stature, a development which is also characteristic of the picaro who "moves horizontally through space and vertically through society."[9]

Lozana, like the female rogue of the seventeenth century, uses her physical assets and practical knowledge to obtain food and clothing and to improve her lot in general. Realizing that her attainment of these material things is dependent on the proper use of her attributes, she remarks: "If I should fail to use these I would die, since I have always heard that only the food which is eaten is beneficial" (V, 46). For Lozana, as for the rogues who take advantage of free meals, astuteness is an indispensable quality which permits survival and even luxuries at the expense of others. When asked by Trigo, the Jewish vendor, to go to visit a wealthy courtesan, Lozana responds positively by saying, "Yes, I will go; it will give me a chance to observe and to experiment and also to eat at other people's expense" (XXII, 107). After all, asks Lozana, "Is there a wiser man than he who knows how to get money from other people's pocket without hard work?" (XV, 82).[10]

Egoism along with a materialistic sense and a perversion of the moral values are traits that are easily discernible in Delicado's protagonist as well as in the picaro. Lozana is an adventuress who acts without scruples because, she tells us, "To need there is no law" (XXIX, 134). What is important to her and to the later picaros is to survive and to succeed in life, to arrive at "the good port," as Lazarillo will say,[11] without any consideration of what is right or fitting. Lozana's positive traits, her beauty, intelligence, and fecund imagination permit her to survive in an adverse world. Her tasks as a courtesan and as a procuress should be seen in the same light as any service performed by the picaros in their search for shelter, clothing, and food and the desire to improve their lot. As in the picaresque tradition, need, ambition, and pleasure are the primary moving forces in Lozana's life. The use of sexual attraction and contrived situations to deceive and ridicule lustful and gullible men and to steal from them is a central motif in most of the picaresque novels with female protagonists.[12] The fundamental philosophy of Lozana and of the protagonists in the other picaresque novels is to deceive and take advantage of those around them in order to live as well as possible.

It is interesting to note that of those corrupted individuals who surround Lozana and of those who come to use her services as a procuress, many praise her for the audacity and astuteness which she displays, not for her being a harlot.[13] An example of this is the comment made by the ambassador who, recalling an earlier encounter with Lozana, tells his friend, the knight: "I saw her in the Bancos district; she talked so pleasantly and with such audacity that she seemed a Seneca!" (XXXVI, 154). In fact, Lozana herself resents being compared to a prostitute (XXXVII, 161); in her eyes and in the eyes of others she is to be distinguished from the masses of courtesans on the basis of her superior physical endowments as well as her intellect and social aspirations. Lozana's goal is not merely to earn a living by using her body and mind to please and deceive others, but also to seek fame by ensuring the integrity of her *honra* ("reputation"). At the beginning of the third part of Delicado's novel, Lozana affirms: "I want to look after my reputation, for, as they say, 'fortune helps the audacious'" (XLI, 172). The association which Lozana makes between her reputation and audacity is significant of her picaresque inclination to interpret success by one's boldness, venturesome spirit, and seductive abilities. Everywhere in Delicado's work we find references to Lozana's ingenuity and audacity, which she repeatedly relates to her ambition to gain the best possible life, in essence, to create a success story.

From the above observations we may deduce that Lozana is, in fact, a proud, greedy, and lustful woman. In this respect she shares yet another similarity with the picaro who, in general, has been considered a compendium of capital sins.[14] Lozana's morality like that of the Spanish female rogues is shaped by the need to use her physical and intellectual attributes; only by doing so can she surmount the hardships of life, fulfill her basic needs, and satisfy her desire to improve her position in society.

Presumption and social ambition are intimately linked with Lozana's pride. Although a daughter of disreputable parents, Lozana strives to ascend the social ladder by changing professions and by attracting a variety of suitors including a cleric, a majordomo, and an ambassador. Lozana's inordinate self-esteem leads her to assert that in spite of her lack of formal education she knows more than the erudite jurists (LX, 228). She takes delight in her achievements, prides herself for her skills as a courtesan and a go-between, and ostentatiously claims to be the most celebrated woman of Rome (XX, 101). Lozana's sense of fame and her presumed refinement find a parallel in the aspirations of Elena, the protagonist of *La hija de la*

Celestina (The Daughter of Celestina, 1612), written by Alonso de Salas Barbadillo.[15]

Lozana's greed can be seen from her earliest association with Diomedes who she hoped was going to be a "perpetual bank" (IV, 44). Following her separation from Diomedes, Lozana's conduct remained fundamentally one of greed as she considered every man she met from the point of view of "what he could give her and what she could swindle from him" (V, 46). In the presence of her victims, Lozana frequently feigns poverty to exhort them to be generous with her (XIX, 96; XXV, 122), and she invariably succeeds. Throughout the work Lozana exhibits a preoccupation for her economic well-being, satiating her ambition by employing astute tricks and deceptions in ways analogous to those used by other well-known female rogues, such as Teresa de Manzanares and Dorotea in the novels of Castillo Solórzano.[16]

The longing and eagerness to be free and enjoy life nourish Lozana's lustful inclinations, as it does in the case of at least six other female protagonists of picaresque novels.[17] Her natural instincts find a propitious ground for development in the erotic world of Rome.[18] The intensity of her inordinate passion is clearly perceived in the bedroom scene with Rampín (XIV, 73 - 76), as well as in several references to aspects of love. ". . . that kiss is worth more than the medal you are wearing on the cap," Lozana tells an infatuated mace-bearer (XIX, 98). After having spent a night of "ecstasy" with the mail carrier, Lozana pleads with him to stay because she does not want to part from "such bliss" (XXII, 105). The passionate ardor which characterizes Lozana is also manifested by other female rogues, among them Justina, the country jilt, who, following an amorous encounter with a man of arms, sees herself burning with passion.[19]

A final point on Lozana as a picaresque character. At the end of the novel, which has an indefinite conclusion, Lozana becomes skeptical of, and disillusioned with, the world around her. Consequently she searches for a change of environment, the island of Lipari, which she hopes will bring her peace and a new life. Symbolically, her action is analogous to that of the best picaros who in the final stage of their vicissitudes decline to react against life's chaotic events and decide instead "to leave the chaos altogether and become a hermit."[20]

In addition to Lozana there is also the impudent Rampín, who can be seen as a precursor of the literary picaro. We will recall that in

Lozana's early efforts to earn a living with her knowledge of cosmetics she seeks the help of Rampín's mother, a shopkeeper. Lozana's apparent familiarity with the beautifying arts impresses the Neapolitan woman who does not hesitate to grant the Andalusian lady's request that Rampín go with her to serve as guide.

One of the basic characteristics of most picaresque novels is that the rogue serves several masters and that in his wanderings he is exposed to individuals of different occupations. For his part Rampín is not a novice at serving masters. In the three months prior to the encounter with Lozana, Rampín had served two masters, a cleric and a squire. The latter, an avaricious and corrupt individual, dismissed Rampín on the mere suspicion that he ate some leftover food (XV, 83). This episode recalls an analogous experience of Lazarillo whose pilfering of his master's wine brings him a memorable punishment. Rampín, like Lazarillo, is the victim of his master's avarice, and the account of his past service is presented with that same satirical spirit that fill the pages of *Lazarillo*.

Rampín, like the picaros after him, grows in a corrupt and cynical world which profoundly shapes his character and contributes to the development of his astuteness and ingenuity. With these attributes he performs successfully a variety of roguish tricks and services which include stealing some shoes as expected payment for his services (XV, 83), delivering messages, and buying cosmetics for the courtesans (XXXI, 138). His precocious experience with the world of the courtesans teaches him to exploit their needs and desires for his own well-being.

There is also a grotesquely humorous treatment of Rampín which reminds us of the characterization of picaros. In memorandum XXXIII there is recorded the episode of Rampín, who, in running away from a big rat, falls into a latrine (p. 143). Later, in memorandum XXIV, he is invited to eat some ham, at the sight and smell of which he vomits "even his intestines" (XXXIV, 149). This incident finds an interesting variation in the episode of *Lazarillo,* in which the young rogue regurgitates a recently stolen piece of sausage.[21] A similar incident is also seen in the *Guzmán de Alfarache,* where the rogue, after eating an omelet of nearly hatched eggs and a piece of black bread, vomits everything.[22]

II *Realism and the Milieu of Delinquency*

From the point of view of novelistic art and ideological intention, the picaresque novel represents a reaction against courtly literature, principally the chivalric romances and the pastoral and sentimental writings in which idealistic, magic, and supernatural elements abound. Contrary to such courtly literature which idealizes nature and provides elegant models for love and courtship, the picaresque novel depicts a wicked and hostile world and the struggle of an individual to survive in it.

In the artistic representation of roguish life some authors, particularly the baroque novelist Quevedo, prompted by the aesthetic values of the time and his violent reaction against the idealism of courtly literature, produced an exaggeration of anti-idealistic materialism, in fact, a grotesque deformation of characters and situations.[23] In most picaresque novels, however, the picaro as well as the other protagonists, and the world around them, are related to a specific reality in time and space and the protagonists' actions characterize them as being concrete and real persons.[24]

It is in this aspect of realism that *Lozana* can be considered an antecedent to the picaresque novel. Episodes and situations in both *Lozana* and the picaresque novel, in general, can be traced to the history of their epoch, and both present social and ethical problems that were of great significance in the Spanish Golden Age,[25] for example, the European wars, the expulsion of the Jews, and the corruption of officials of the law and of the Church.

Realism in *Lozana* and in the picaresque novel is characterized also by the sketches of manners and of individuals of various social classes and professions encountered by the protagonist.[26] *Lozana* offers us a true "observatory" of life as it pertains to the libertine Roman society, and we can properly repeat what Erich Auerbach has noted in connection with the banquet scene in the *Satyricon* that "nothing is left mysteriously in the background, everything is expressed."[27] Such artistic concern must have also been in the mind of Mateo Alemán whose *Guzmán de Alfarache* carries the subtitle of *Watchtower on Human Life*.

An integral part of *Lozana* and of the novel of roguery is the atmosphere of delinquency: rogues, vagabonds, charlatans, pretentious nobles, and corrupted clerics (VII, 50; XIV, 77; XXII, 107; XXXII, 140).[28] The stage of *Lozana,* the decadent world of Renaissance Rome, is analogous to the degenerate scenario on which the picaresque novel comes to life. It has been said that the most important example of the picaresque genre, *Guzmán de Alfarache*, reflects a society in progressive decadence and on the verge of collapse.[29] We can make a similar observation about *Lozana,* where social corruption and libertinism are seen as the cause not only of much physical suffering but also of the destruction that befell Rome in 1527.

III *Humor*

"The classical rule of the separation of styles, which became influential in the sixteenth century, stipulated in practice that everything pertaining to everyday life — social classes and occupations, the common events of life in real places actually named and described — had to be written in the 'low style', which meant that in theory it could not be treated on any level except the comic."[30] Alexander Parker reminds us that in theory this "presupposed narrow boundaries for realism, since the comic excluded any serious treatment of a serious problem."[31] In fact, however, some of the best Spanish picaresque novelists, we are told, succeeded in showing that literature can be "both truthful and morally responsible."[32] Delicado, a precursor of the picaresque novelists, shares with such writers as Quevedo and Cervantes the literary triumph of treating realistic subjects with a serious interest in the problems of everyday life. We have seen how Delicado's ostensible intention of creating a faithful portrait of Roman life is linked to his morally didactic purpose of showing the foibles of human existence. His opulent use of comic scenes taken from life are entertaining, to be sure, but they are also thought-provoking for they reflect the magnitude of man's blindness to his destiny. The reader wishes to be entertained, and Delicado, like the picaresque novelists, gives him a chance to laugh away his sadness and suffering.[33] We will recall Delicado's view of *Lozana* as a work intended to alleviate the affliction of those who, like himself, had fled Rome under the fear of death and had now settled in Venice. The entertaining picture of the carefree life and jovial days of Rome will bring back happy memories to his Venetian readers but it will also make them aware of the futility of those delightful times.

In addition to reproducing comic scenes from contemporary life, Delicado frequently manipulates language artistically for humorous purposes. Alliterations and puns as well as ironic and metaphorical expressions abound in *Lozana,* as for example, *cocho* ("cooked," "expert in love"), *asado* ("roasted," "tight," "virgin") (IV, 42); *trintín [tin tin] y botín* ("clink of metal and booty," "money") (XX, 102); *tercera* ("third on the guitar," "procuress") (XXI, 104); *alcuza de santero* ("bottomless well," "insatiable woman") (XXIV, 119). Unfortunately, the meaning of the wordplay in these and other examples is usually lost in the English translation.

Humor in *Lozana* goes beyond verbal effects; it is also used as an instrument of satire, burlesque, caricature, and parody.[34] Delicado's use of comic satire to denounce, with a didactic purpose, the social abuses of his times, is a technique that was widely adapted by the writers of picaresque novels as well.[35] Jokes, stories, and anecdotes in *Lozana* and in the picaresque novel capture the attention of the reader so that he may become gradually exposed to the negative aspects of its society, and learn something from it. In spite of Delicado's contention that his work is devoid of things pertaining to clerics and the church, *Lozana* contains several humorously ironic and satirical references to religious figures. This we have already observed in chapter 6. With regard to social satire, this is mainly directed to the nobility.

As we have seen in the previous chapter, the episode in which the protagonist instructs the young Coridón on the ways to make himself acceptable to the beautiful Polidora is a good example of satire of the high social classes for their lofty and pretentious ideals. For Lozana it is quite apparent that in the actual life of sixteenth-century Rome there is no room for the courtly "suffering," there is only the reality of joyous and physical companionship. Moreover, the world of the nobility is burlesqued in an ironical reference by Rampín's aunt to Rome as the *tierra de Cornualla* ("land of Cornwall") (XIV, 73), the celebrated land of knightly heroes; the reference is a pun, for in roguish jargon the Spanish word *Cornualla* actually means "cuckold." Humor as an instrument for satirizing the nobility is also seen in a dialogue between Lozana and the vagabond Sagüeso, who asserts that the courtesan Celidonia enjoys a greater reputation than she. Lozana, distressed with Sagüeso's opinion, reacts by saying: "They [Celidonia and the other courtesans] may surpass me in money and opulence but not in lineage or blood." With an obvious intent to ridicule the system of differentiating nobility from the other classes, on the basis of lineage and blood, Sagüeso gives a humorously ironic reply: "I bet you are right; but just to be sure, it will be necessary to bleed both of you to see who has better blood" (LII, 200).[36] The dialogue between Lozana and Sagüeso is not only humorously sarcastic toward the social system in general, but it is also related to a specific sociohistorical preoccupation of the converso. Lozana's selfishly motivated nature, her skillfull efforts to succeed in life, to underline her supremacy among the courtesans, and to affirm her nobility of blood are clearly related to the converso's frustrated idealism and to his desire for *hidalguía* ("nobility"), as is manifested in the picaresque novels.

Two eminent historians and literary critics, Américo Castro and Marcel Bataillon, have presented very convincing theories that the picaresque novel is intimately linked with the social problem of the Jew and the converso in Spain.[37] For almost two hundred years following the political unification of Spain, in 1492, the only Spaniards to enjoy full social rights were the *cristianos viejos,* or "old Christians," whose dignity and status depended on their freedom from the slightest taint of Jewish or Moorish blood. Under such conditions of unreasoning prejudice the conversos were repressed, and as a result of their inferior social condition many of them reflected a subconscious desire for nobility of blood. Artistically, this is seen in *Lazarillo,* for example, where the protagonist's first act upon the attainment of economic security is to purchase a sword, symbol of respectability and of traditional nobility. Historically, however, the inability to cope with social prejudices and their own failures, resulted in an attitude of frustration and general despair among the conversos, who frequently acquired a negative view of life and a rancorous attitude toward its values. It is in this anguish of the religious convert of Spain that Américo Castro sees the origin of the picaresque novel.[38]

Bataillon's study of the picaresque novel's relationship to the converso has been very likely enriched by his careful scrutiny of the satire motif in *La pícara Justina* (Justina: The Country Jilt), a picaresque novel written by Francisco López de Úbeda and published in Medina del Campo, in 1605. A significant part of Professor Bataillon's analysis of *Justina* revolves around the protagonist's consistent attacks against those who display an obsessive preoccupation with honor, reputation, and genealogical background. Frequently in the work, Justina, the daughter of innkeepers, ridicules impoverished and proud nobles and spurious nobles in high positions. Ultimately, however, when she finds herself at the peak of her picaresque success, she, too, begins to acquire a spirit of nobility,[39] thereby becoming herself the object of ridicule, as does Lozana.

The above considerations have shown, then, another important connection between Delicado's work and the picaresque novel. In the true picaresque tradition, Delicado uses humor as an expression of realism and as an instrument of satire for the purpose of teaching a moral lesson.

IV *The Episodic Plot*

Another of *Lozana*'s characteristics that later becomes an integral aspect of the picaresque novel is its episodic plot. The narration and dialogue in *Lozana* record a series of fragmented episodes. Each memorandum registers the events surrounding different individuals and situations. The fundamental unity of *Lozana*, as of the picaresque novel, derives the presence of the main protagonist, who serves as the link between the episodes, a central theme, and a uniform interpretation of life.[40]

V *Conclusion*

Although *Lozana* cannot be properly called a picaresque novel, it does exhibit several characteristics that later become an integral part of the novel of roguery. In contrast to the ideal and fantastic world depicted in courtly literature, Delicado's work, like the picaresque novel, reflects a world of material needs and recognizable geographical places. In a form analogous to that of the picaresque novel, *Lozana*'s components are historical, urbane, erotic, and adventurous; the external frame is picturesque and descriptive;[41] the characters are numerous and representative of various social classes. The satire of corrupt individuals, customs, and manners is didactically oriented. Similarly, the author interjects amusing episodes with the ultimate purpose of moral censure.

Lozana and the world around her are depicted in a succession of scenes that is reminiscent of the episodic plot of the picaresque novel. The main protagonists, Lozana and Rampín, like the picaros, are the product of the lower and disreputable class of society; they have no scruples, and they rely on their ingenuity and wit to live in an adverse world and to exploit others. Lozana, like most female rogues, is linked with pride, deceit, greed, and sex. The picaresque motif of the change of masters is exemplified by Rampín.

CHAPTER 8

El modo de adoperare el legno de India occidentale
(On the Use of the West Indies' Wood)

I *The Front-Piece Woodcut*

THIS booklet consists of fifteen pages written in gothic letters, and is illustrated with two woodcuts, one on the title page and the other in folio seven recto. The front-piece woodcut, which occupies almost the entire page, is immediately under the title. At the center of the woodcut is represented the therapeutic West Indies' wood or "holy wood" crowned by the Blessed Virgin holding the symbolic pilgrim's staff and having the image of Santiago (Saint James) on one side and of Saint Martha with the palm of martyrdom on the other. Saint Martha is also restraining the ferocious *tarasca*, the serpent's figure borne in the Corpus Christi procession, which is devouring a child by the banks of the river Rodamus. Of great interest to us in this first woodcut is the figure of a cleric kneeling before Saint James, with the inscription: *Francisco Delicado composuit in alma urbe, anno 1525* ("Francisco Delicado composed it in the holy city in the year 1525"), which signifies that it is probably a portrait of the author. He is seen as a relatively short man with a trimmed beard, a receding hairline, and an afflicted facial expression. With his hands joined in the act of praying, he has a dagger in his chest, symbolic of his suffering.

II *Structure and Summary*

Delicado's treatise on the West Indies' wood can be divided into five parts: (1) dedication; (2) description of the "French disease," its origin, and the prescription for its cure; (3) letter of Fernández de Oviedo; (4) epilogue; and (5) papal proclamation. The treatise is dedicated to three Italian professors of medicine — Juan Bautista Papiense, Domingo Senno, and Julio Marciano Rota. In the dedication, written in Latin, Delicado expresses his admiration for these illustrious physicians and acknowledges his gratitude for their sup-

[103]

port. He also affirms that the writing of the treatise was not motivated by a search for glory, but rather by his desire to alleviate the suffering of those who, like himself, became victims of syphilis. Delicado also speaks of the concomitant severe pains of this disease, which he endured for twenty-three years.

Written in Italian, because "there are more of those who do not know Latin," the second part of Delicado's treatise begins with a description of the origin of the venereal plague, which corresponds to that given by Divicia in *Lozana,* already discussed in chapter 5. For Delicado, a Spaniard, the blame for this great social evil rests on the French, although we should note "that the lexicological history of venereal disease in Spain as elsewhere, reveals ... a constant effort to shift to other nations the responsibility for the social scourge which struck Europe at the end of the fifteenth century."[1]

What follows the discussion of the origin of the "French disease" is a rather detailed explanation of the discovery of the curative *leño guayaco* ("guaiacum wood"), its properties, and the way to administer it. This wood is from a tree described as having the height of the ash tree, with leaves somewhat rounder and larger than those of the arbutus. Its yellowish fruit, resembling in size two small dates joined together, had been used by the Indians to cure elephantiasis, and Spanish sailors, infected with the *bubas* (pustules caused by venereal disease), found that the same fruit could also be used to cure their infirmity. Later, the wood itself, with its siccative property, was discovered to be beneficial to those suffering from the disease. For therapeutic purposes, Delicado prescribes a mixture of the sawdust from this wood and oil of hipericon which, after boiling, was to be used to anoint the sores. By combining the content with an equal amount of water, the mixture would then be taken internally *bis in diem* ("twice a day"). To the ailing patient, Delicado also recommends daily exercises, a gradual reduction of food intake, and a diet which consists largely of fruit. The aforesaid treatment was to last forty days, excluding ten days for convalescing, and the cure was designed for men between the ages of fourteen and sixty.

In his treatise on this wonder drug of the sixteenth century, Delicado is systematic and precise. He presents a very informative historical account of the discovery of the West Indies' wood, its diffusion in Spain (1508) and in Italy (1517); and, in a most detailed manner, he introduces an empirical remedy for the venereal plague of the time. In all, this is an extremely interesting Renaissance document on medicine, history, and language, as well as an important

El modo de adoperare el legno [105]

source of information about its author, whose humanitarian concern led Pope Clement VII to call him *dilectus filius* ("esteemed son").

The seriousness of this social evil as well as the trend to combat it with this Caribbean wood is also reflected in the writings of the famous natural historian, Gonzalo Fernández de Oviedo, whose important letter on the *palo santo al qual los indios llaman guaiacán* (holy wood which the Indians call guaiacum) is reproduced in the third part of Delicado's treatise. The letter, as found in Delicado's essay, corresponds substantially to the text of Fernández de Oviedo's *Historia general y natural de las Indias* (General and Natural History of the Indies), published in Toledo in 1526, and brought to Italy by the Venetian ambassador to Spain, Andrea Navagero. In this very extensive work we find some of the most informative descriptions of Indian customs as well as keen observations on the fauna and flora of the West Indies. The part of the text on the "holy wood" which Delicado reproduces contains a number of variants which, however, do not alter the basic history of this wood nor its traditionally accepted curative properties as described by Fernández de Oviedo.

The fourth part of Delicado's treatise consists of the epilogue, which, unlike the preliminary pages, is written in Spanish "because the discussion of this wood gives much prestige to our Romance language." It is directed "to all those who had, have, or will have, the incurable disease," and its moral tone reminds us of the final pages of *Lozana*. The description of destruction and suffering created by the simultaneous appearance of war and plague once again colors the artist's work with a distinct shade of sadness. Citing the biblical words against the wicked and the blasphemers from the books of Psalms and Revelation, Delicado makes specific reference to the cruel and merciless deeds committed by foreign soldiers on Italian soil during the French takeover of Rapallo in 1480 and during the Spanish sack of Rome by the troops of Charles V in 1527. Delicado's treatise ends with a papal proclamation of Clement VII which bears the date of December 4, 1526. In the proclamation, Delicado is given a ten-year copyright for his booklet which is acknowledged as a remedy to those suffering from the disease of the "Gallic pustules."

III *Critical Observations*

Ours are the paintings, ours are the sculptures, ours is wisdom, ours are . . . all the inventions, . . . ours are, at last, all the marvelous and almost incredible discoveries which the power and the insight of human genius wants to make and edify. (Poggio Bracciolini, *Letters*, VII, 1)

The vital and exuberant spirit of the Renaissance, which the Italian humanist Poggio Bracciolini expresses majestically with the above words, denotes man's new vision of himself and of the world around him. This new vision animated art, literature, philosophy, and education; and it led to geographical discoveries and new inventions. Scientific experimentation designed to increase man's knowledge of himself and to improve and heal his physical being can be seen in Leonardo da Vinci's penetrating analysis of the human body and in Paracelsus's studies of medicinal remedies to cure various diseases. It can also be observed, specifically, in the treatises dealing with syphilis, then known by a variety of names, as we have mentioned in chapter 5.

Known to the civilized world since the end of the fifteenth century, syphilis became the object of study for many Renaissance humanists. The first scientific account of the disease is that provided by Gaspar Torella in his treatise *De pudendraga sive morbo gallico* (On Genital or Venereal Disease, Rome, 1497). The earliest historical discussion of this *Gallic disease* is found in the work of Nicolaus Leonicemus, *De epidemia quam Itali morbum gallicum vocant* (On the Sickness Which the Italians Call Gallic Disease, Venice, 1497). In Spain, the first clinical document of this disease was that written by the physician Villalobos, in his *Sumario de la medicina . . . con un tratado sobre las pestíferas bubas* (Summary of Medicine . . . with a Treatise on the Pestiferous Pustules, Salamanca, 1498). In 1514 Juan de Vigo described with great accuracy the stages of the disease in his *Pratica Copiosa in Arte Chirurgica* (Complete Manual of Surgical Arts), published in Rome.

Francisco Delicado was undoubtedly familiar with some of the above writings as is reflected by the fact that, while in Italy, he published at least two already-mentioned treatises on the subject. Of *On the Use of the West Indies' Wood* there exist two known copies: one, at the Marciana Library of Venice; the other, at the Mazarine Library of Paris. According to the colophon, they were published in Venice on February 10, 1529, and are very likely revisions of an earlier edition published probably in Rome in 1526. The author alludes to this when, on folio 7 verso of the Venetian edition, he says, "I did not include in this second edition the composition of the electuary. . . . I shall include it in the third." The place and date of the

El modo de adoperare el legno

presumed earlier edition can be deduced from the papal letter of Clement VII, found on the last folio of the 1529 edition. We may rightly presume that because of its medical value, the initial reception of this treatise was indeed notable and its importance acknowledged by excellent physicians of the time, such as those to whom the work is dedicated.

The importance of this essay of Delicado continued to be evident in the eighteenth century when Jean Astruc, eminent professor of medicine at Montpellier and Paris, provided a résumé of Delicado's treatise in the second edition of his well-known work *De morbis venereis* (On Venereal Pustules), published in Paris in 1740. Later, the Spanish Jesuit Francisco Xavier Lampillas made use of Astruc's Latin résumé in his *Saggio storico-apologetico della letteratura spagnuola* (Historico-Apologetic Essay of Spanish Literature, Genoa, 1778 - 81), in which he distinguishes Francisco Delicado among the Italian physicians for his contribution to the knowledge of the medicinal and curative properties of the West Indies' wood.

In the nineteenth century, Delicado's unique treatise received further attention from such figures as Antonio Hernández Morejón in his *Historia bibliográfica de la medicina española* (Bibliographical History of Spanish Medicine), cited in chapter 5, and by his contemporary, Anastasio Chinchilla, in the very informative *Anales históricos de la medicina* (Historical Annals of Medicine, Valencia, 1841). Hernández Morejón and Chinchilla, like a number of other lesser known historians of medicine of that period, continued to view Delicado as a foremost physician and specialist in venereal diseases.

It was not until *Lozana* was brought to light in 1875 that Delicado received recognition as a man of letters. Curiously enough, some encyclopedic collections have had two separate entries for Francisco Delicado, one in which he is seen as a literary figure and the other as a physician, without mentioning any relationship between the two. An excellent example of this apparent confusion can be found in the *Nouvelle biographie générale* (New General Biography), published in Paris by Didot in 1866, in which François Delicado appears as a Spanish man of letters, for his edition of *Primaleón* (Venice, 1534), and, under a separate listing, as a priest, doctor, and author of the treatise on the West Indies' wood.

At the turn of the century, however, with the studies of Menéndez Pelayo[2] and Benedetto Croce,[3] the figure of Francisco Delicado as both man of medicine and of letters became somewhat more clearly delineated. Croce, in fact, refers to Delicado as "physician and scholar,"[4] and in almost all subsequent studies on Delicado, he is given some recognition for his contributions to the healing arts as well as to the world of letters. Yet, it is significant that, with the exception of Joaquín del Val,[5] no one has, until now, provided an adequate description and study of Delicado's *On the Use of the West Indies' Wood*, his greatest known contribution to the history of medicine and an important source for the author's biography.

IV Conclusion

In conclusion, Delicado's treatise received prompt recognition for its great humanitarian value, and its importance in the history of medicine has continued to be acknowledged since the appearance of its résumé in Jean Astruc's *De morbis venereis* (On Venereal Pustules). This work of Delicado, however, is also important for the autobiographical information which it contains. First of all, the author's physical appearance, merely alluded to in *Lozana*, is more clearly disclosed in the portrait which appears on the title page. Second, Delicado's extensive suffering from the venereal plague of the time, mentioned in *Lozana*, can be more adequately understood by his disclosure of having endured its severe punishment for twenty-three years. Third, the extent of the author's knowledge of the Italian language, scantily reflected in some linguistically mixed dialogues of his novel, becomes more apparent in the systematically presented thoughts of his treatise.

Besides the importance which this work of Delicado has had in the history of medicine and the useful autobiographical information which it provides, the treatise is also helpful in determining more convincingly the extent of Delicado's influence on his contemporaries, especially on the Italian humanist Pietro Aretino. In the following chapter it will be shown that, considering the notable influence which Spanish writers had on Italian literary productions of the sixteenth century, we cannot deny the possibility that Delicado's *Lozana* inspired, in effect, the creation of the *Ragionamenti* (Discussions, Venice, 1533, 1536) by Aretino. It is very probable that both Delicado and *Lozana* had been known to Aretino, who lived in Rome at the beginning of the sixteenth century and moved to Venice in the same year as did Delicado. Like *Lozana*, Aretino's work is a vivid representation of the corrupt and licentious Renaissance society. The *Discussions*, besides depicting various scenes of the Roman prostitution with the same background found in *Lozana*, also mentions a number of bawds and harlots found in the pages of the

El modo de adoperare el legno

Spanish novel. And a further aspect common to both works is the presence of lively dialogues rich with ironic expressions and exotic words.

The idea of Aretino's indebtedness to Delicado, first suggested by Apollinaire,[6] acquires even greater support in light of the fact that the description of the "French illness" and of the ways to combat it as found in the treatise on the West Indies' wood is also directly imitated by the Italian writer. This is reiterated by Manzella Frontini when she asserts that "without any doubt we can affirm that Aretino translated directly the pages of Francisco Delicado, including even those passages dealing with the advice to the poor victims of the disease based on the remedy indicated and discovered by Delicado."[7] In essence, then, these considerations should prove the very significant point that Delicado was not an obscure author, as maintained by Menéndez Pelayo, and that his writings, rather than being an isolated and uninfluential product of Spanish letters, left a notable mark on the literary creation of Pietro Aretino and, very possibly, on other humanistic writers.

CHAPTER 9

Delicado and Aretino: Aspects of a Literary Profile

I Historical Perspective

TO study objectively Francisco Delicado and Pietro Aretino and to evaluate their literary creations one must view the artists and their works within the framework of sixteenth-century humanism. The cinquecento, remarks Arturo Graf, "is profoundly immoral and the magnitude of its immorality can be measured by the boundless space which separates the real life from the Christian ideal."[1] Since the primary objective of Delicado and Aretino was to depict vividly the "real life" of the Renaissance world in which they lived, their merits, as artists, should be assessed by their success in portraying that life, irrespective of our views on its "immorality"[2] and its detachment from a Christian ideal.

The major reason for which, until recently, Delicado and *Lozana* have received so little attention in the world of Spanish letters and for which Aretino has been considered an infamous idol of pornographic literature is that both men have been the victims of puritanical historians and critics, chief among whom are Menéndez Pelayo[3] and Francesco De Sanctis.[4] Because of these critics' adverse opinions, Delicado's work, like his name, became associated with licentiousness and corruption in the way that the name Aretino came to be a symbol of turpitude and wickedness.

II Biographical Facts

Much more is known, of course, about the life of Aretino than that of Delicado, whom we know only through the remarks which he and his characters make in the pages of his writings. On the other hand, information about Aretino abounds, both in his works and in the opinions of his contemporaries.[5] All evidence points to the fact that Aretino, like Delicado, was largely a self-educated man[6] in search of profit,[7] that he led a libertine life,[8] and that, most importantly, his ambition as a writer rested in his desire to portray realistically the world around him.⁹

III *Artistic Similarities*

A literary profile of the writings of both men reveals a striking similarity in the artistic representation of the same model: the world of Renaissance Rome. As we mentioned in chapter 2, the similar nature of their literary compositions, noticed very shortly after the discovery of *Lozana*, led the Marqués de la Fuensanta del Valle and José Sancho Rayón to assert that Delicado's work was a direct imitation of Aretino's *Ragionamenti* (Discussions). This, of course, could not be, since, as Alcide Bonneau first noted, the publication of the *Discussions* was later than that of *Lozana*, and if there were an imitator, the French scholar asserts, it would be Aretino, not Delicado. This possibility of seeing Aretino as the imitator was rejected, however, by Menéndez Pelayo, who felt that "in such matters Aretino did not need to receive lessons from anyone, much less from the obscure author of *Lozana*, whom no one cites in Italy or in Spain during that century."¹⁰ In this respect, Menéndez Pelayo is in agreement with the Italian critic Arturo Farinelli, who states: "It is questionable . . . that Aretino fashioned the *Discussions* and the *Puttana errante* (Wandering Harlot) on the type of the impudent and clever *Lozana*. . . . In the licentious life of the courtesans and brothel women, Aretino, an expert in everything, knew a bit more than Delicado . . . nor does it seem to be that *Lozana*, even though written in Rome, was well known at the time to Aretino."¹¹ The extent of this polemic was further augmented when Guillaume Apollinaire proceeded to go beyond the question of imitation and attributed the very authorship of a part of the *Discussions*, the *Dialogo dello Zoppino* (Dialogue of Zoppino), to Delicado, and not to Aretino as had been originally thought.¹² It is true that Apollinaire's arguments for the attribution of *Zoppino* to Delicado are inconclusive, but they serve to underline, nevertheless, the traditional awareness of the existence of profound similarities between the literary artistry of Pietro Aretino and Francisco Delicado.

The Eternal City, which forms the background to the narratives of Delicado and Aretino, unfolds before us in a similar manner. We have already seen in chapters 5 and 6 how accurately and naturally Rampín proceeds to show Lozana the Roman surroundings. In *La Cortigiana* (The Courtesan), Aretino's first play (Rome, 1524),

Maestro Andrea has a function analogous to that of Rampín, as he introduces Messer Maco to the Roman locale:

Messer Maco. What is the Colosseum?
Maestro Andrea. The treasure and the consolation of Rome. . . . ah, let's go to see the mausoleum . . . the business street of Banchi, and the tower of Nona.
Messer Maco. What church is this?
Maestro Andrea. Saint Peter; enter with reverence.

Messer Maco. Il Culiseo che cosa è?
Maestro Andrea. Il tesoro e la consolazion di Roma. . . . ah, andiamo a veder Campo santo . . . Banchi, torre di Nona.
Messer Maco. Che chiesa è questa?
Maestro Andrea. San Pietro, entrateci con divozione.[13]

This technique by which the setting is gradually and vividly disclosed before us is also seen in another of Aretino's plays, *The Talanta* (Venice, 1542), where Ponzio, a Roman, reveals to Messer Vergolo, a Venetian, the sites of the Eternal City:

Messer Vergolo. Well, what is that thing so large and so majestic?
Ponzio. It used to be called the Pantheon, built by Agrippa, and now it's called the Ritonda, and it is the most beautiful temple ever built.
Messer Vergolo. What is that one called that is half ruined and looks like the whole world?
Ponzio. The Colosseum. . . .
Messer Vergolo. That long beam made of strange stones, and pointed on top, what is it called?
Ponzio. The obelisk, and in the golden ball which you see on top are contained the ashes of Julius Caesar.

Messer Vergolo. Bè, che cosa è quella così grande e così grossa?
Ponzio. Si chiamava già il Panteon edificato per Agrippa, et ora è detta la Ritonda, et è il più bel tempio che mai si facesse.
Messer Vergolo. Come si chiama quello che così mezzo rovinato pare tutto il mondo?
Ponzio. Il Coliseo. . . .
Messer Vergolo. Quella baia lunga di pietra strana, accantonata et aguzza in la punta, come ha nome?
Ponzio. La guglia, e ne la palla indorata, che gli vedete sopra, son le ceneri di Giulio Cesare.[14]

These parts of Rome also form the setting for the scurrilous dialogues of Aretino's *Discussions*. From the rather confined world of the first day of the *capricciosi ragionamenti* ("Whimsical discussions") dealing with convent life, Aretino soon transfers his narrative to the streets where the scenes become alive with color and sound. On the third day Nanna describes to Antonio her first view of Rome: "We arrived on the eve of St. Peter. You can't imagine the pleasure I felt in seeing the rays of light and the fireworks and hearing the music coming from the castles, from the districts of Ponte, Borgo, and Banchi."[15]

IV *The Libertine Protagonists*

Besides projecting their narrative against this common background of sixteenth-century Rome with its well-known quarters of Banchi, Borgo, and Ponte Sisto, the above-mentioned works of Aretino and *Lozana* provide us with a second aspect of similarity — the lascivious nature of their protagonists. Lozana, deprived of the necessities of life, quickly develops the practice of a variety of minor celestinesque arts, as well as her major role as a prostitute and procuress. With "*arte e ingenio*" ("art and ingenuity") she soon becomes a successful courtesan. Confidently she remarks to the mail carrier: "Perhaps there is no other woman in Rome who has been more courted than I" (XX, 101). In fact, references to her success as a courtesan are frequent in the novel, and the companion summarizes it well when he affirms, "there is no man who doesn't want to go to bed with her at least once . . . " (XXIV, 114). In this respect, Lozana reminds us of Alvigia in Aretino's *The Courtesan*, who proudly distinguishes herself from the other courtesans: "In my times, neither Lorenzina . . . nor Angioletta of Naples nor Beatrice . . . nor that famous Imperia were fit to take off my shoes, and all those servants and maids were rubbish compared to me."[16] A similar portrait of the successful courtesan is also presented in *The Talanta* and in the *Discussions*, where Nanna, herself a renowned harlot, teaches her daughter Pippa the arts needed to excel in the profession. The result here as well as in *Lozana* is a detailed picture of the Roman prostitution around which revolves a countless number of pleasure-seeking individuals: servants, squires, soldiers, and clerics.

V *The Satirical Intention*

The appearance of such diverse social types in the works of Aretino and Delicado lends itself well to the sharp satire directed against the whole of a pretentious, abusive, and corrupt society. In this social intention we find another point of resemblance between the writings of Aretino and Delicado. Commenting on this aspect of

The Courtesan, Gino Lanfranchi remarks that in writing his play Aretino's intention was to create "a formidable satire of the life in Rome, filled then with hypocritical and perverse courtiers, immoral prelates, greedy and rapacious pimps, scoundrels of every sort, buffoons, and thieves."[17] Aretino's contempt for these social parasites is evident in *The Courtesan* as well as in the pages of *The Talanta*[18] and the *Discussions*,[19] where the satirical intention becomes even more piercingly effective. An identical portrait of Roman corruption is also seen in *Lozana*, in which Delicado satirically describes the general social decay and provides a picture of Roman prostitution equalled only by the writings of Pietro Aretino.

VI *Form and Style*

A profile of the artistic creations of Delicado and Aretino reveals not only a remarkable similarity of content, but also an equally notable likeness of form, providing yet another aspect common to the writings of the two authors. In complete harmony with Delicado's intention to portray, to reproduce faithfully, the "nature" around him, the structure of *Lozana* is based on the lively dialogue which is also intrinsically characteristic of Aretino's *Discussions* as well as of such plays as *The Courtesan* and *The Talanta*. The stylistic art of Delicado, like that of Aretino, lies in his ability to reproduce the dialogue, the spoken words of those who move through the streets and piazzas of Rome. Arturo Graf commented that "Aretino's goal is to be able to translate with words the plastic quality of things, the intensity and the fervor of life. . . ."[20] The result is that the writings of Aretino, as well as *Lozana*, provide us with a rich source of linguistic usages and idiomatic expressions of the time. Like Bartolomé de Torres Naharro in his plays *Soldadesca* and *Tinelaria*, Delicado and Aretino capture the totality of the language with its jargon, Latinisms, neologisms, and foreign expressions common to the heterogeneous communities of sixteenth-century Italy.

VII *Sensuality and Morality*

A further similarity between Aretino and Delicado can be seen in the fluctuation between the sensual and the spiritual, or moral, which exhibits itself so clearly in their literary creations. While producing some of the most vivid descriptions of licentiousness in the *Discussions* and in his plays, Aretino also treats a variety of religious and moral themes in his *Prose sacre* (Sacred Prose). These spiritual writings, which include a treatise on the "Humanity of Christ" and an exposition of biblical mysteries, have traditionally been seen, at best, as the product of Aretino's artistic assimilation and as a work completely devoid of a genuine religious feeling. For the Italian critic Giuseppe Toffanin, for example, the *Sacred Prose* represents nothing more than Aretino's interest in displaying his mastery of word-painting, "always Pietro's strong point in literary composition."[21]

Admittedly, Aretino, as a literary painter, is as successful in his treatment of spiritual themes as he is in the description of the world in which he lived, but his religious highlights may not be dismissed as a mere exercise in pictorial rhetoric. As a recent authoritative biography of Aretino shows, he always remained a good Catholic at heart, if not in conduct.[22] This would make it not at all unreasonable to accept Giorgio Petrocchi's view that Aretino's ascetic writings emanated from the spirit of the Counter Reformation. Further, at the time in which Aretino was sketching some of his religious topics in Venice, the Adriatic city was a center of Thomistic studies, used then as a major instrument of defense of the Counter-Reformation. In fact, one of Aretino's best written saints' lives, the *Vita di San Tommaso d'Aquino* (Life of Saint Thomas Aquinas), which is a part of his *Sacred Prose*, underlines the author's responsiveness to the ecclesiastical needs of the time as well as his unfeigned religious feeling.[23] This dualistic aspect of Aretino's sentiments, reflected by his creation of the *Discussions* on the one hand and of the *Sacred Prose* on the other, also manifests itself in Delicado whose *Lozana* combines a sensual portrait of pleasure with a recurring moral motif.

As we have already observed, *Lozana* was published in Venice in 1528, months after Delicado had sought refuge there, following the sack of Rome. Prior to having his work published, however, he revised it; and, in the process, the lively and often risqué dialogues of his novel became interspersed with a series of prognostications of the imminent destruction of Rome, which color the portrait with a distinct moral tone. And it would seem a reasonable conjecture to think that in this process of "revision" the author wanted to underline the moral significance of *Lozana* by introducing in the final pages of the novel the protagonist's disillusionment with life.

A final note on Delicado's moral intention can be seen when, viewing the sack of Rome in retrospect, the author closes his novel with a vivid description of the chaos and destruction which befell the Eternal City, reiterating that the sack and its accompanying suffering was a divine punishment of the sinful inhabitants of Rome: "Oh, God! Who would ever have thought of such divine decree and judgment as this which this year befell the inhabitants that offended You? . . . Oh, how much grief followed your liberty and your lack of restraint, Rome, for not wanting to moderate your ingratitude for so many benefactions received!" (Epilogue, 253). Delicado's work ends with this morally evocative tone, and, in this light, the final pages of the novel complement well the ostensible didactic intention of the author. Thus, whereas Aretino displays his dualistic sentiments toward the sensuous and the moral in distinct works, Delicado juxtaposes them in the same literary creation.

VIII Conclusion

In conclusion, then, Francisco Delicado and Pietro Aretino have long been subjected to the misguided judgment of critics who, prevented by their prejudices from noticing the artistic merits of these writers, condemned them and their literary creations as immoral and pornographic. Of Aretino, the Italian critic Francesco De Sanctis said that "a decent man would not utter that name before a lady."[24] Menéndez Pelayo shared this feeling not only for Aretino but also for Delicado, whose life and works he studied, as he asserts, only because of his duty as a literary historian. As we have seen, however, to judge these writers properly it is necessary to view them and their literary creations within the framework of the Italian cinquecento. To determine the literary accomplishment of Delicado and Aretino we should study the extent to which both authors succeed in their ostensible intention to portray realistically and faithfully the world in which they lived.

A literary profile of *Lozana*, the *Discussions*, and the above-mentioned plays of Aretino reflects unquestionably the authors' success at creating a literary painting of the life of Renaissance Rome. The great merit of the works of Delicado and Aretino is "naturalness." Their characters, in lively dialogues, make us hear the sounds of the charlatans as we move with them about the Roman quarters; they show us the brothels and teach us the secrets of the courtesans; and it is all presented with the utmost veracity of detail, much like a report written by an experienced journalist who strives to capture the sights and sounds of a particular event. On this aspect of the artistry of Aretino, Graf concluded that the Italian writer "felt the need for an art which was intimately connected with life, and which would draw inspiration and breath directly from life. According to him, the poet must keep the eye fixed on nature, not on the models; he must live with nature, in a vital and continuous communion; he must learn his art from it."[25] Because of his professed intention to create a portrait based only on what he "heard and saw," it is apparent that Delicado also sought in nature the inspiration and the essence of his art.

As has been pointed out, a further similarity between the works of Delicado and Aretino is the satirical intention which prevails in their literary portraits. According to Garnett,[26] satire was first exercised in gibing at personal defects, and with later advance in literary art it became dignified as an instrument of morality. Although it is true that Aretino as a satirist was interested in attracting attention to himself and in securing some sort of impregnable political, social, and financial position, there can be no doubt that the Italian writer, like Delicado, had an important function in making known the political and social abuses and evils of Renaissance Rome, thus preparing the way for their eventual modification. This belief is consistent with Marc Kanzer's view[27] that the appearance of such writers as Cervantes, Voltaire, and Gogol on the national scene in their respective cultures and ages could be thought of as warnings of latent revolutionary forces, which the works of these satirists notably stimulated.

In most of Aretino's work we find a tendency to comment satirically on political affairs and on the misconduct of high officials, including the clerics of whom he wrote frequently in a clearly burlesque vein. In *The Courtesan*, the comic character Maco, a simple fellow, goes to Rome with the intention of becoming a cardinal. The painter Andrea, a cynic, informs him that in order to become a cardinal he must first become a courtier, and subjects him to a variety of humiliating and degrading situations, which, he informs Maco, are necessary to attain that end. The burlesque technique is also employed by Delicado in his treatment of clerics, as can be seen in the dialogue between Lozana and Rampín, cited in chapter 6. As we have seen, however, satire in the works of Delicado and Aretino encompasses not only the criticism of the nobility and of clerics for their misconduct and pretentiousness, but also that of lascivious women, gullible men, courtiers, and servants of all types, for their deceitfulness and greediness.

We have seen, also, that another aspect common to the literary creations of Francisco Delicado and Pietro Aretino is the basic dualism reflected by the occurrence of, and the fluctuation between, the sensual and the moral — a tension so frequent in the man of the Renaissance. In *Lozana* Delicado presents concurrently a faithful portrait of Roman sensuality and his personal moral interpretation of human intemperance. Pietro Aretino, on the other hand, never displays this basic dualism within the same literary creation, but rather he offers us distinct works in which we either find depicted the most vivid sketches of Renaissance wantonness, as in the *Discussions*, or some of the best treatments of religious and spiritual themes, as in the *Sacred Prose*. Considered by a few critics as the frankest pornography in Italian literature, the *Discussions* and some of Aretino's plays are, instead, works of literary value in the artistic representation of Renaissance Rome, and they are of sociological relevance as important historical documents of the time. The licentiousness of these works comes from the reality of the world in which the author lived. In the prologue to *The Courtesan*, Aretino writes: "If I fail to observe the usual order that comedy demands, do not be surprised at it, because one lives in another manner in Rome than in Athens."[28] Aretino, like Delicado, was most intimately concerned with reproducing, in the form of a literary painting, the world around him with all its sensuality and lasciviousness; this literary aspiration, however, does not preclude the possibility that the writer possessed a genuine religious feeling, as seen in his movingly expressive *Sacred Prose*.

CHAPTER 10

Summation

AT the beginning of this century, Menéndez Pelayo complained that Delicado was an unlearned man and that his work did not follow the guidelines established by literary tradition. This, of course, is not true, as we have attempted to show in this study. Besides, "works of art are not created according to theory; rather, theories are made according to works of art."[1] The Swiss playwright Friedrich Dürrenmatt notes that the artist has no need of scholarship. "Scholarship derives laws from what exists already; otherwise it would not be scholarship. But the laws thus established have no value for the artist, even when they are true."[2]

The adverse criticism which attacked *Lozana* for its so-called immorality has no legitimate basis. What does exist in some of its passages is, as María Rosa Lida de Malkiel so aptly indicates, a certain "jocose obscenity,"[3] a sensuality which produces, in the words of another scholar, "a smile at the mature man."[4] Those who have so vehemently censured Delicado's work have missed seeing that the "sensual intoxication" of Roman society is represented with a distinct tone of artistic comicality, explicitly created to divert our attention from the crudeness of the model to the realization of the human folly with which man seeks momentary pleasures.

Living in exile, Delicado assimilated much of what Renaissance Italy had to offer, although he retained a profoundly Spanish mentality. This is seen in *Lozana,* a work which reflects some of the most intrinsically Spanish characteristics: picturesqueness and a deep sense of humor, a realistic treatment of common events, persons and emotions of daily life, and a fundamental preoccupation with man's destiny. The novel is conceived as a biography of a woman known to the author and as a social chronicle of Renaissance Rome. As such, the work is a valuable historical and sociological document of the Renaissance courtesans, of venereal disease, and of the Jewish and converso community of Rome. *Lozana,* however, is not a mere historical document, it is a work of art designed to entertain as well as to teach a moral lesson. To entertain, Delicado takes certain scenes of contemporary life and treats them with humor, wit, and irony. Like the poet for whom "the sound must seem an Echo to the senses,"[5] Delicado chooses a language that is totally compatible with the comic effect he is seeking, as in the amorous scene between Lozana and Rampín. To instruct, he shows the disillusionment and the physical suffering that follows those amorous encounters, so blindly sought by his protagonists.

In basing his novel on the immediate reality that surrounds him, Delicado ingeniously and vividly depicts authentic scenes from life in a living language rich in colloquialisms and proverbs. The successive enumeration of places and historical events enliven the portrait in the same way in which the "proximity and contemporaneity" of the events sung by the narrator give verisimilitude to the Castilian epic.[6] Together with a profoundly vivid view of life in Renaissance Rome, Delicado gives us his personal interpretation of that life. Looking at the corrupt Roman society, in retrospect, Delicado, like his protagonist, moralizes on human folly. It is the realization of the futility of human endeavors that moves Delicado to God and Lozana to the pursuit of peace.

With regard to *Lozana's* relationship to subsequent literature, we have noted its affinity with the picaresque novel. Unlike the chivalric and pastoral romances where the heroes triumph in an idealized utopian world of fantasy, *Lozana* and the picaresque novel present an individual whose success is judged in terms of his ability to survive in a real and dissolute society. Lozana, the exuberant Andalusian woman, lives in the reality of that world from which she takes, with astuteness and ingenuity, whatever she needs to succeed in life and to retain her freedom. She learns from experience that deceit and trickery are indispensable weapons for success. In a way similar to the rogue, Lozana is a vagabond but also a philosopher. In the course of her vicissitudes she sees a variety of places and she meets several individuals of different social classes. The observation of pretentiousness and social abuses leads her to comment critically on the human condition and to reflect on its vanity.

For his realistic treatment of life and for his uninhibited study of human nature Delicado can be considered a precursor of the modern novelist. Like the modern realist writer, Delicado convinces us completely that the events of his novel are occurring at a particular place

Summation

and at a particular time, and our memory of *Lozana* consists largely of those vividly realized moments in the lives of its characters.[7] Delicado's use of the *mamotreto,* as a "memorandum" or a "notebook," finds an interesting parallel among several nineteenth-century writers, including the philosopher Kierkegaard. The critic Bertil Romberg has shown how in his novel *Skyldig-Ikke Skyldig* (Guilty-Not Guilty) Kierkegaard skillfully employs the diary device: "Here, every morning, the narrator notes down in his journal everything that happened one year before on the day in question, while at midnight he writes up the events and thoughts of the present day."[8]

In spite of the strong objections which early twentieth-century critics raised against *Lozana* for its "immorality," some modern writers are likely to have appreciated its art. Pío Baroja, for example, whose own works read much like diaries, must have looked with interest on the almost cinematographic presentation of the subject matter in *Lozana,* a work which he cites in his *El árbol de la ciencia* (The Tree of Knowledge).[9]

Ortega y Gasset observes that "The upper level of the novel is a tragedy. . . .The tragical line is inevitable; it must form part of the novel, if only as the very thin edge which limits it."[10] The tragic thread in *Lozana* is spun from the folly with which man seeks pleasures and worldly vanities, and it ends with the disillusionment of the protagonist and the emotionally tragic notes of the destruction of a decadent society besieged by vice. The total structure of *Lozana* is oriented in the direction of this moral lesson and of the realistic representation of Renaissance Rome.

Notes and References

Chapter One

1. Francisco Delicado, *Retrato de la lozana andaluza,* ed. Bruno M. Damiani (Madrid: Castalia, 1969), pp. 187 - 90. Unless otherwise noted, all subsequent textual references to *Lozana* will be taken from this edition.
2. See Francisco Márquez Villanueva, "El mundo converso de *La Lozana andaluza,*" to appear soon in *Archivo Hispalense.*
3. Otis Green, *Spain and the Western Tradition: The Castilian Mind in Literature from "El Cid" to Calderón* (Madison, Milwaukee, and London, 1968), III, 55.
4. "La Garza Montesina," in *Obras Completas de Alfonso Reyes* (Madrid, 1917), VI, 249 - 56; Alfonso Reyes, "Un enigma de *La Lozana,*" in *Homenaje a Dámaso Alonso* (Madrid, 1960), III, 151 - 54.
5. It is a work cited by Antonio Palau y Dulcet in his *Manual del librero hispanoamericano* (Barcelona, 1951), IV, 349.
6. *La Lozana andaluza,* ed. Joaquín del Val (Madrid: Taurus, 1967), p. 22.
7. Annamaria Gallina, "L'attività editoriale di due spagnoli a Venezia nella prima metá del '500," *Studi Ispanici* I (1962), 69.
8. Benedetto Croce, *La Spagna nella vita italiana durante la rinascenza* (Bari: Laterza, 1949), pp. 164 - 65.
9. Annamaria Gallina, *op. cit.,* p. 69.
10. Annamaria Gallina, *op. cit.,* pp. 69 - 80. Cfr. *Libros de caballerías,* ed. Pascual de Gayangos (Madrid: Rivadeneyra, 1857), pp. XXXIX - XL. Edwin Place's edition of the *Amadís* (Madrid: *Consejo Superior de Investigaciones Científicas,* 1971), I, xx. Apparently, however, Daniel Eisenberg does not share Gallina's views on Delicado's merits as an editor; see his review of my edition of *La Lozana andaluza, Hispanófila* 46 (1972), 79 - 80.
11. Amado Alonso, *De la pronunciación medieval a la moderna en español* (Madrid: Gredos, 1967), p. 112.
12. Amado Alonso, *op. cit.,* p. 115.
13. Annamaria Gallina, *op. cit.,* p. 76.

14. Amado Alonso, *op. cit.*, pp. 115, 155 - 56, 312.
15. Amado Alonso, *op. cit.*, p. 112.
16. Marcelino Menéndez Pelayo, *Origenes de la novela*, ed. Enrique Sánchez Reyes (Santander: *Consejo Superior de Investigaciones Científicas*, 1943), IV, 54.

Chapter Two

1. The Spanish adjective *lozana* means "lusty," "luxuriant," "sprightly."
2. Ferdinand Wolf announced the discovery in his article "Ueber das spanische Drama; *La Celestina* und seine Uebersetzungen," in *Blättern für literarische Unterhaltungen* (Berlin, 1845), nn. 213 - 17, pp. 853 - 70. The article was later reproduced in Wolf's *Studien zur Geschichte der spanischen und portugiesischen Nationalliteratur* (Berlin, 1859), pp. 278 - 302.
3. While editing Delicado's Venetian edition of the chivalric romance *Amadis*, Gayangos found a reference to Delicado's authorship of the work, made by Delicado himself in his prologue to the *Amadis (Libros de caballerías*, ed. Pascual de Gayangos, in *Biblioteca de autores españoles*, 40 [Madrid, 1857]), p. 7.
4. *La Lozana andaluza*, ed. Marqués de la Fuensanta del Valle y José Sancho Rayón (Madrid, 1871), pp. VII - VIII ff. *La Lozana andaluza*, ed. Alcide Bonneau (Paris, 1888), pp. XI - XII ff.
5. Bonneau, *op. cit.*, p. XII.
6. See *La Lozana andaluza*, ed. Antonio Álvarez de la Villa (Paris, 1900), p. 4 ff.
7. Marcelino Menéndez Pelayo, *Orígenes*, IV, 54, 57 - 61. Cf. Peter Dunn's review of my *Lozana* edition, in *Bulletin of Hispanic Studies* 48 (1971), 158 - 59.
8. *Op. cit.*, p. 54 ff.
9. Manzella Frontini, *La Lozana andaluza* (Catania, 1910), pp. VI ff; *La Lozana andaluza*, ed. Guillaume Apollinaire (Paris, 1912), p. 15 ff.
10. Antonio Álvarez de la Villa, *op. cit.*, p. 7.
11. *La Lozana andaluza*, ed. José Gómez de la Serna (Santiago de Chile, 1942), p. 8.
12. *Ibid.*, pp. 11, 13, 15.
13. The facsimile edition was made by Antonio Pérez Gómez (Valencia, 1950).
14. See the Bibliography.
15. *La Lozana andaluza*, ed. Antonio Vilanova (Barcelona, 1952).
16. *Ibid.*, pp. XI - LI.
17. Antonio Vilanova, "Cervantes y *La Lozana andaluza*," *Insula*, May 1952, n. 77, p. 5.
18. Bruce Wardropper, "La novela como retrato: el arte de Francisco Delicado," *Nueva revista de filología hispánica* 7 (1957), 475 - 88. Years before Wardropper presented his illuminating interpretation of Delicado's

novel as a portrait, Alfonso Reyes had perceived Delicado's literary technique which he referred to as the product of "a master in the art of portrayal" (Alfonso Reyes, "La Garza Montesina," *Obras completas,* VI, 253).

19. Segundo Serrano Poncela, "Aldonza la andaluza Lozana en Roma," *Cuadernos Americanos* 122 (1962), 117 - 32.

20. Christo Thomas Mocas, "Aspectos lexicográficos de *La Lozana andaluza*" (Ph.D. diss., Tulane University, 1954).

21. Lester Beberfall, "Italian influences on the Partitive Indefinite Construction in the *Lozana Andaluza*," *Italica* 32 (1955), 108 - 113; *idem,* "Some Italian Influences in Delicado's *La Lozana Andaluza,*" *Hispania* 49 (1966), 828 - 30.

22. Manuel Criado de Val, "Antífrasis y contaminaciones de sentido erótico en *La Lozana andaluza,*" in *Homenaje a Dámaso Alonso* (Madrid, 1960), I, 431 - 57.

23. Albert Ian Bagby, Jr., " 'La Lozana andaluza' vista en su perspectiva donjuanesca," *Hispanófila* 35 (1969), 19 - 25.

24. José Antonio Hernández Ortiz, "La originalidad artística de *La Lozana andaluza*" (Ph.D. diss., Yale, 1971). The relationship of *Lozana* with Erasmian writings had been briefly mentioned earlier by Antonio Vilanova *(op. cit.,* p. XX) and Nicasio Salvador Miguel ("En torno al *Retrato de la Lozana Andaluza,*" *La Estafeta Literaria* [1967], n. 373, p. 12).

Chapter 3

1. Menéndez Pelayo, *Orígenes,* IV, 57.

2. Lane Cooper, ed. *Aristotle: On the Art of Poetry* (Ithaca, 1967), pp. XX, XXIV - XXXV; Marcelino Menéndez Pelayo, *Historia de las Ideas Estéticas en España* (Madrid, 1962), II, 391. To understand the supremacy of nature as an artistic model of the Renaissance, see Robert Clemens, *Michelangelo's Theory of Art* (New York, 1961), pp. 402 ff.

3. Otis Green, *op. cit.,* III, 278.

4. Aristotle, *Nicomachean Ethics,* I, 5.

5. John Herman Randall, *Aristotle* (New York, 1960), pp. 244 ff; see also William Hardie, "The Final Good in Aristotle's *Ethics,*" in *Aristotle: A Collection of Essays,* ed. Julius Moravcsik (University of Notre Dame Press, 1967), pp. 298 - 301.

6. See Bruce Wardropper, "*La novela como retrato* . . . ," p. 477.

7. See Persius, *Satirae,* II, verses 31 - 34; V, verse 185 ff.

8. "Epistola enim non erubescit" ("because a letter does not blush") Cicero, *Epistulae,* V, 12, 1.

9. Seneca, "Veritatis simplex oratio est" (*Epistulae,* 49, 4). Seneca was a classical figure well-known in Spain since the thirteenth century. In the juridical work of Alfonso el Sabio, Seneca is mentioned as "the philosopher from Cordova" (Partida II, Title IV, Law # 2). In Law # 4 Seneca is also

cited. In his doctoral dissertation Hernández overlooks this point, as he comments that Seneca's Hispanic origin began to be recognized only in the second half of the fifteenth century (*op. cit.*, p. 178). Cf. Jacob Burckhardt, *The Civilization of the Renaissance in Italy* (New York: Harper, 1958), II, 478. The indebtedness of the authors of celestinesque novels to Seneca is discussed in a study by Joseph Heller and Raymond Grismer, "Seneca in the Celestinesque novel," *Hispanic Review* 12 (1944), 29 - 48.

10. In conjunction with Demosthenes, Delicado also mentions Aeschines, the orator's perpetual rival, whose famous words about his compatriot *Quid si ipsam audissetis bestiam* ("Well, what would it be if you had heard the monster himself"), are given in the preliminary pages of *Lozana* (ed. Damiani, p. 36).

11. Menéndez Pelayo, *Orígenes*, IV, 244 - 263.

12. Observations made by Hernández, *op. cit.*, pp. 179 - 82.

13. This episode had already appeared in the German pseudopicaresque tales of *Till Eulenspiegel*.

14. Juan Ruiz, *Libro de Buen Amor*, ed. María Brey Mariño (Madrid: Castalia, 1966) p. 39, couplet 13.

15. On this topic see the fine articles of John Strong Tatlock, "Mediaeval Laughter," *Speculum* XXI (1946), 289 ff., and Helen Adolf, "On Mediaeval Laughter," *Speculum* XXII (1947), 251 ff.

16. *Libro de Buen Amor*, ed. cit., p. 47, couplet 65.

17. Mario Marti, *Cultura e stile nei poeti giocosi del tempo di Dante* (Pisa, 1953), p. 213; Marti's opinion is also cited by Otis Green, *Spain and the Western Tradition*, I, p. 30.

18. Diego Sánchez de Badajoz, in the Introit to his *Farsa Teologal*, cited by Otis Green, *op. cit.*, I, 27.

19. *Libro de Buen Amor*, ed. Joan Corominas (Madrid: Gredos, 1967), p. 162, note to verses 374 ff.

20. Kenneth Scholberg, *Sátira e invectiva en la España medieval* (Madrid: Gredos, 1971), p. 150. The corresponding parts of the text are found in stanzas 372 - 87.

21. *Libro de Buen Amor*, ed. Brey Mariño, pp. 96 - 98, couplet 490 - 513.

22. María Rosa Lida de Malkiel, *Two Spanish Masterpieces: The Book of Good Love* and *The Celestina* (Urbana: The University of Illinois Press, 1961), pp. 24 ff.

23. *Libro de Buen Amor*, ed. Brey Mariño, p. 48, couplet 71.

24. For a detailed study of the antifeminist tradition in Spain, see Jacob Ornstein, "La misoginia y el profeminismo en la literatura castellana," *Revista de filología hispánica* III (1941), 219 - 32.

25. Angel Valbuena Prat, *Historia de la literatura española* (Madrid, 1960), I, 284. Valbuena Prat also refers to Martínez de Toledo as "the observer of life" (*op. cit.*, p. 285).

26. *El Corbacho*, ed. Lesley Byrd Simpson (Berkeley, 1939), p. 7.

27. *Ibid.*, p. 145.

28. *Ibid.*, pp. 291 - 92. Joaquín González Muela comments on the

Archpriest of Talavera's ability to produce a literary painting in which he records all that he sees and hears; in *Corbacho,* ed. González Muela (Madrid: Castalia, 1970), pp. 18, 26 - 27, 29.

29. Dámaso Alonso, "El arcipreste de Talavera a medio camino entre moralista y novelista," in *De los siglos oscuros al de oro* (Madrid: Gredos, 1958), pp. 125 - 36.

30. Edward Fueter, *Histoire de l'historiographie moderne* (Paris, 1914), p. 112, cited by Ramón Iglesia in *Cronistas e historiadores de la conquista de México* (Mexico, 1942), pp. 101 - 2, note.

31. Fernán Pérez de Guzmán, *Generaciones y semblanzas,* ed. Jesús Domínguez Bordona (Madrid, 1924), p. 8.

32. *Ibid.,* p. 5, cf. *'Propalladia' and Other Works of Torres Naharro,* ed. Joseph Gillet (Bryn Mawr: Banta, 1951), IV, 226 - 27.

33. Hernando del Pulgar, *Claros varones de Castilla* (Madrid: Clásicos Castellanos, 1923), p. 6. For a very fine study of Pulgar's artistic technique see José Luis Romero, "Hernando del Pulgar y los claros varones de Castilla," in his *Sobre la biografía y la historia* (Buenos Aires, 1945), pp. 153 - 69.

34. Domínguez Bordona, *op. cit.,* p. XX.

35. The reference is to a well-known passage dealing with the princes of Carrión who fled, shamefully, from a lion. See *Romancero general,* ed. Agustín Durán (Madrid, 1945), I, 542 - 43.

36. See Ramón Menéndez Pidal, *Flor nueva de romances viejos* (Buenos Aires: Espasa Calpe, 1963), pp. 202 - 3.

37. Luigi di Francia, *Franco Sacchetti novelliere* (Pisa, 1902), pp. 166 - 76.

38. See María Rosa Lida de Malkiel, "Función del cuento popular en el *Lazarillo de Tormes*" (*Actas del primer congreso internacional de hispanistas,* Oxford, 1963), p. 350, n. 4; on the folkloric tradition of *Lazarillo,* see Marcel Bataillon, *Novedad y fecundidad del Lazarillo de Tormes* (Madrid: Anaya, 1968), pp. 27 - 45.

39. See Adolfo de Castro, ed., *Crónica de Don Francesillo de Zúñiga* (Madrid: 1855), *Biblioteca de autores español*es, vol. XXXVI, 38.

40. See Cervantes, *Comedias y entremeses,* ed. Rudolf Schevill and Adolfo Bonilla y San Martín (Madrid, 1922), VI, 141.

41. See Francesillo de Zúñiga, *Epistolario,* ed. Adolfo de Castro (Madrid: 1855), *Biblioteca de autores españoles,* vol. XXXVI, 55.

42. See Gonzalo de Correas, *Vocabulario de refranes y frases proverbiales* (Madrid, 1924), pp. 253, 598; Joseph E. Gillet, "Traces of the Wandering Jew in Spain," *Romanic Review* 22 (1931), 16 - 27; Marcel Bataillon, "Pérégrinations espagnoles du juif errant," *Bulletin Hispanique* 43 (1918), 81 - 122.

43. Cf. Marcelino Menéndez Pelayo, *Estudios sobre el teatro de Lope de Vega* (Santander, 1949), IV, 401 - 21.

44. Cf. *Diccionario de la lengua española* (Madrid: Real Academia Española, 1947), *s.v. judío.*

45. See Ramón Rozzell, "The Song and Legend of Gómez Arias,"

Hispanic Review 20 (1952), 91 - 107.

46. Menéndez Pelayo observes that the cited passage is one of the first evidences in favor of the tradition which sees Salamanca as the setting of *Celestina (Orígenes*, IV, 55).

47. See Stephen Gilman's comments on the "spoken word" in the *Celestina*, "Diálogo y estilo en la *Celestina*," *Nueva revista de filolgía hispánica* 7 (1957), 461 - 69.

48. Benedetto Croce, *La Spagna nella vita italiana durante la Rinascenza*, pp. 115 - 36.

49. Anna Krause, "The Sentimental Novel" (Ph.D. diss., University of Chicago, 1928), p. 151.

50. *Ibid.*, p. 143.

51. *Ibid.*, p. 143, note 2.

52. Observation which is made by Hernández, *op. cit.*, pp. 63 - 64. Cf. *Diálogo de la lengua*, ed. Juan Lope Blanch (Madrid: Castalia, 1969), p. 10. See Juan Luis Vives, *Introducción de la sabiduría*, ed. Marian Leona Tobriner (New York, 1968), pp. 46 - 74, where Vives's Renaissance themes and his views on the literary imitation of reality are discussed.

53. *Propalladia, ed. cit.*, I, 143.

54. "Just as the *Soldadesca* is the first picture of military life in literature, the *Tinellaria* is the first play to show life below stairs in a Roman palace of the Renaissance" (*Propalladia, ed. cit.*, IV, 513; see also pp. 509 - 16). See Bartolomé de Torres Naharro, *Comedias Soldadesca - Tinelaria - Himenea*, ed. Dean William McPheeters (Madrid: Castalia, 1973), pp. 17 - 26. The artistic goal which Naharro proposes to attain in his *Comedia Soldadesca* is discussed by María Rosa Lida de Malkiel, "El fanfarrón en el teatro del Renacimiento," *Romance Philology* XI (1958), 274 - 75.

55. Lucretia, the washerwoman in *Tinelaria*, reappears with some of the same characteristics in *Lozana, ed. cit.*, pp. 65 - 69. See also the views on Rome presented by Torres Naharro in his poetry, in *Propalladia, ed. cit.*, I, 161 - 65.

56. Joseph Gillet suggests that "a modern reader would be likely to marvel" at Torres Naharro's mentioned artistic ability, with respect to act 3 of *Tinelaria*, whose large number of characters present at one time was seen by Moratín as producing confusion (*Propalladia*, ed. Gillet, IV, 514). It appears to me that Professor Gillet's words can also be applied very appropriately to Delicado's reaction, not only to that act of the *Tinelaria* but to Naharro's other very fine plays, as well. The whole of Rome, as depicted by Naharro and Delicado, is a "scene of turbulence."

57. Delicado's familiarity with this work is evidenced also by Divicia's knowledge of the brothel of Valencia where she had worked (p. 202). This brothel is the setting for many of the *Song Book's* stories.

58. *La comedia Thebaida*, ed. George Douglas Trotter and Keith Whinnom (London: Tamesis, 1968), p. XXXIV. In the introduction to this superb edition of *Thebaida, Professor Whinnom discusses perceptively the literary*

merit of the work which, like *Lozana,* had traditionally received adverse judgment for being an inferior imitation of *Celestina* and for its "immorality." See my review of this edition in *Modern Language Notes* 88 (1973), 417 - 21.

59. *Comedia Seraphina* in *Colección de libros españoles raros o curiosos,* ed. Marqués de la Fuensanta del Valle y José Sancho Rayón (Madrid, 1873), pp. 379 - 80.

60. Menéndez Pelayo, *Orígenes,* IV, 54 - 58.

Chapter Four

1. See Bertil Romberg, *Studies in the Narrative Technique of the First-Person Novel* (Stockholm: Almquist, 1962), p. 61.

2. Clayton Hamilton, *Materials and Methods in Fiction* (New York: Baker and Taylor, 1908), p. 129.

3. Bertil Romberg, *op. cit.,* p. 15.

4. Bruce Wardropper, "La novela como retrato . . . ," p. 477.

5. Wardropper, *op. cit.,* p. 480.

6. José María Díez Borque, "Francisco Delicado, autor y personaje de *La Lozana andaluza,"* *Prohemio* 3 (1972), 463.

7. Percy Lubbock, *The Craft of Fiction,* in *Perspectives on Fiction,* ed. James Calderwood and Harold Toliver (New York, London, and Toronto: Oxford University Press, 1968), p. 231.

8. In *Writers at Work, The Paris Review Interviews,* ed. Malcolm Cowley (New York, 1958), p. 55.

9. Díez Borque, *op. cit.,* p. 464.

10. Donald McGrady, *Mateo Alemán* (New York: Twayne, 1968), p. 78.

11. Antonio Prieto, *Ensayo semiológico de sistemas literarios* (Barcelona: Planeta, 1972), p. 77; José María Díez Borque, *op. cit.,* p. 463.

12. Antonio Prieto, *op. cit.,* p. 77.

Chapter Five

1. Bruce Wardropper, "La novela como retrato . . . ," p. 475; Menéndez Pelayo, *Orígenes,* IV, 54; *La Lozana andaluza,* ed. Antonio Álvarez de la Villa, pp. 257 - 58.

2. García Márquez, in his review of my edition of *La Lozana andaluza,* in *Triunfo,* n. 417, May 30, 1970.

3. In Esteban Eccard, *Corpus historicum medii aevi* (Rome, 1894), II, 1997. On the great number of courtesans living in Rome, see *La Lozana andaluza, ed. cit.,* p. 131.

4. Domenico Gnoli, "La Lozana andaluza e le cortigiane nelle Roma di Leon X," *Nuova Antologia* VII (1931), 177.

5. *Ibid.*

6. Mariano Armellini, *Un censimento della città di Roma sotto Leone X* (Rome, 1882), IV, 40 ff.
7. Domenico Gnoli, *op. cit.,* p. 178, note 41.
8. Pietro Aretino also describes the licentious milieu of these districts in his *Ragionamenti* (Discussions) and in the *Dialogo dello Zoppino*. Luca Contile, a contemporary of Aretino, gives further details on the subject (*La Pescara* [Milano, 1550], p. XIX).
9. For the history of this very interesting district of Rome, see Maria Teresa Russo, "Una contrada di Roma sparita: appunti di topografia," *Strenna dei Romanisti* 29 (1968), 327.
10. Maria Teresa Russo, *op. cit.,* p. 333.
11. Maria Teresa Russo, "Pozzo Bianco nella finzione letteraria e nella realtà," *L'Urbe* 24 (1962), 23.
12. *Propalladia, ed. cit.,* III, 415. Also see Umberto Gnoli, *Topografia e toponomastica di Roma Medioevale e moderna* (Rome, 1939), p. 244; Ludovico Pastor, *Storia dei papi dalla fine del medio evo . . .*, (Rome, 1926), VI, 264.
13. Maria Teresa Russo, "Pozzo Bianco . . . ," p. 21.
14. "Pozzo Bianco . . . ," p. 22.
15. *Propalladia, ed. cit.,* III, 496; cf. Guillaume Apollinaire, *L'oeuvre du divin Aretin* (Paris, 1909 - 1923), I, 33.
16. Domenico Gnoli, "Cortigiane della Rinascenza," *Vasari* (1940), pp. 5 - 39; 66 - 84; 107 - 28. Cf. Pio Pecchiai, *Roma nel Cinquecento* (Bologna, 1948), pp. 311 - 12.
17. *Propalladia, ed. cit.,* III, p. 511. Cf. Henry Rushbury, *Rome of the Renaissance and Today* (London, 1932), p. 130.
18. Armellini, *op. cit.,* pp. 52 ff; Gnoli, "Descriptio Urbis," *Archivo della Società Romana di Storia Patria,* 17 (1894), 375 - 520.
19. Cf. Pio Pecchiai, *op. cit.,* pp. 313 - 14; Alfonso Reyes, "Un enigma de La Lozana andaluza," p. 153.
20. Segundo Serrano Poncela, "Aldonza la Andaluza Lozana en Roma," p. 123.
21. Cesare Vecellio, *Habiti antichi et moderni di tutto il mondo* (Venice, 1598), pp. 25, 26, 107, 114, 203; Cf. Arturo Graf, *Attraverso il Cinquecento* (Torino, 1926), p. 197.
22. Niccolò Franco, *Le pistole vulgari* (Venice, 1542), folio 223v; cf. Arturo Graf, *op. cit.,* pp. 203 - 4.
23. See Pio Pecchiai, *op. cit.,* pp. 308 - 9.
24. Graf, *op. cit.,* pp. 197 - 206.
25. Alfonso Reyes, "La Garza Montesina," p. 250.
26. Alfonso de Valdés, *Diálogo de las cosas ocurridas en Roma,* ed. José Montesinos (Madrid: Clásicos Castellanos, 1928), p. 143.
27. Joseph Gillet, *op. cit.,* III, 260.
28. Cf. Ludwig Pfandl, *Cultura y costumbres del pueblo español de los*

Notes and References

siglos XVI y XVII (Barcelona, 1942), pp. 172 - 73; also see Samuel Gili Gaya, *Tesoro lexicográfico* (Madrid, 1947), I, *s.v. buba.*

29. Gillet, *op. cit.,* III, 260; also see p. 250.

30. Among the first treatises was Gaspar Torella's *De pudendraga sive morbo gallico* (Rome, 1497); cf. also Sebastian Aquilanus, *De morbo gallico* (Rome, 1517).

31. *La pícara Justina,* ed. Julio Puyol y Alonso (Madrid: *Sociedad de bibliófilos madrileños,* 1912), III, 184 - 85.

32. Sebastián de Horozco, *Cancionero,* ed. *Sociedad de bibliófilos andaluces* (Seville, 1874), pp. 1 - 4.

33. *La pícara Justina,* ed. cit., pp. 25 - 27. Also see Marcel Bataillon's excellent historicocritical evaluation of this work, *Pícaros y picaresca* (Madrid: Taurus, 1969).

34. Jack Weiner, "El 'Santo Grillimón' en un poema del *Cancionero* de Sebastián de Horozco," *Hispanófila* 49 (1973), 11 - 16.

35. *Ibid.,* p. 13. It was common at the time to laugh at deformed people in general and to ridicule the victims of syphilis, in particular; see Miguel de Cervantes, *El casamiento engañoso y el coloquio de los perros,* ed. Agustín de Amezúa y Mayo (Madrid, 1912), p. 413.

36. Weiner, *op. cit.,* p. 15.

37. The work was published in Madrid in 1842 - 52; see vol. I, pp. 363 - 91.

38. Gonzalo Fernández de Oviedo, *Historia general y natural de las Indias* (Toledo, 1525). See the edition of Juan Pérez de Tudela y Bueso in *Biblioteca de autores españoles* (Madrid, 1959), vols. 117, 121.

39. Rafael Alberti, *Teatro* (Buenos Aires: Losada, 1964), pp. 10 - 11.

40. Gonzalo de Correas, *Vocabulario de refranes* . . . , p. 246.

41. Menéndez Pelayo, *Orígenes,* IV, 57.

42. *Ibid.,* p. 58.

43. The subject of the Jews and the *conversos* is one which has attracted the attention of a number of distinguished Hispanists, among them, Antonio Domínguez Ortiz (*La clase social de los conversos en Castilla en la Edad Moderna,* Madrid, 1955); Albert Sicroff (*Les controverses des statuts de "Pureté de sang" en Espagne du XVe au XVIIe siècle,* Paris, 1960); and Caro Baroja (*Los judíos en la España moderna y contemporánea,* Madrid, 1961). The complex *converso* problem is carefully studied by Francisco Márquez Villanueva, who assesses it in terms of the social and religious aspects of Spanish life, the *limpieza de sangre* ("purity of blood") mania, which involved proof of Christian lineage, and the Inquisition ("The *converso* problem: an assessment," in *Collected studies in Honour of América Castro's 80th Year,* ed. M. P. Hornik [Oxford, 1965], pp. 318 - 33).

44. See Julio Caro Baroja, *Los judíos en la España moderna y contemporánea* (Madrid, 1961) I, 244 - 245.

45. Francisco Márquez Villanueva, "El mundo converso de *La Lozana*

andaluza," to appear in *Archivo Hispalense.*

46. See, for example, Américo Castro, *De la edad conflictiva* (Madrid, 1961), pp. 149 - 60.

47. See Charles Aubrun, "Conversos del siglo XV (a propósito de Antón de Montoro)," *Filología* 13 (1968 - 1969), 59 - 63.

48. See Ruth Pike, "The *Conversos* in *La Lozana Andaluza,*" *Modern Language Notes* 84 (1969), 306. The mentioned document has been published by Claudio Guillén, "Un padrón de conversos sevillanos," *Bulletin Hispanique* 65 (1963), 49 - 89.

49. Ruth Pike, *op. cit.,* p. 306. See also Antonio Domínguez Ortiz, "Los conversos de origen judío después de la expulsión," *Estudios de historia social de España,* ed. Carmelo Viñas Mey (Madrid, 1955), III, 361 - 71; Mark Wischnitzer, *A History of Jewish Crafts and Guilds* (New York, 1965), pp. 114 - 24.

50. Salo Wittmayer Baron, *A Social and Religious History of the Jews* (New York: Columbia University Press), II, 15. See also Cecil Roth, *The History of the Jews in Italy* (Philadelphia, 1946), p. 68.

51. Cf. Américo Castro, *Cervantes y los casticismos españoles* (Madrid and Barcelona, 1966), pp. 17 - 18.

52. Francisco Márquez, "El mundo converso de *La Lozana andaluza."*

53. Mark Wischnitzer, *op. cit.,* p. 123.

54. Cecil Roth, *op. cit.,* p. 179.

55. *Ibid.,* p. 180.

56. *Ibid.,* p. 187.

57. *Ibid.,* pp. 174 - 274.

58. *Ibid.,* p. 1.

59. *Ibid.,* p. 329.

60. Rafael Lapesa, *Historia de la lengua española* (Madrid, 1962), p. 338. I wish to acknowledge the above-mentioned article of Professor Márquez on the "Conversos in *La Lozana andaluza"* in which he cites the same textual reference calling attention to my incorrect accentuation of the word *Dío* in my edition of *Lozana.*

61. Roth, *op. cit.,* pp. 193 - 227.

62. *Ibid.,* pp. 180, 183, 223.

Chapter Six

1. René Wellek and Austin Warren, *Theory of Literature* (New York: Harcourt, Brace and World, 1956), p. 94.

2. *Ibid.,* p. 104.

3. Menéndez Pelayo, *Orígenes,* IV, 54, 57; Eugenio Asensio, "Juan de Valdés contra Delicado . . . ," 109.

4. Joaquín Casalduero, *Sentido y forma de las novelas ejemplares* (Madrid: Gredos, 1969), p. 67.

5. "So for the Aristotelian, form in a work of art is not structure (in a narrow sense) alone, but all that determines specific character, meaning or expressiveness, as well as structure, in a formal element. (But meaning, besides possessing structure and conferring it, since it involves relation, is itself a kind of structure.) Actually, the Aristotelian will find in a work of art not one form but many, a complexity of formal elements or formalities (structures and meanings), the totality of which is the form (the structure, the meaning, the character) of the work as a whole" (Joseph Shipley, *Dictionary of World Literature* [Boston, 1970] pp. 127 - 28).

6. See chapter 3, note 4.

7. The term "Renaissance spirit" is used here to denote the liveliness, exuberance, and libertinism that prevails in the work. Cf. Américo Castro, "Algunos temas de la *Celestina*," in his *Santa Teresa y otros ensayos* (Madrid, 1929), pp. 203 - 15; Manuel Criado de Val, *De la Edad Media al Siglo de Oro* (Madrid, 1965), p. 109; Lorenzo il Magnifico, *Trionfo di Bacco e Arianna*, in *Scrittori d'Italia*, ed. Natalino Sapegno (Florence, 1963), I, Arturo Graf, *op. cit.*, p. 88.

8. Wellek and Warren, *op. cit.*, p. 121.

9. For the various meanings of *bemol*, see Juan Mir y Noguera, *Rebusco de voces castizas* (Madrid, 1967), *s.v. abemoladamente, bemol;* Rafael Suárez, "Metáforas musicales en el idioma castellano," *Modern Language Journal* 33 (1949), 179 - 84.

10. Hernández, "La originalidad artística de *La Lozana andaluza*," pp. 59 - 71.

11. Charles August Van Rooy, *Studies in Classical Satire and Related Literary Theory* (Leiden: Brill, 1965), p. 104.

12. See Alberto Porqueras Mayo, *El prólogo como género literario* (Madrid 1957), pp. 22 - 23; George Kennedy, "The Earliest Rhetorical Handbooks," *American Journal of Philology* 80 (1959), 169 - 78; also by George Kennedy, "The Rhetoric of Advocacy in Greece and Rome," *ibid.* 89 (1968), 419 - 36.

13. Cf. José Sánchez, "Nombres que reemplazan a capítulo en libros antiguos," *Hispanic Review* 2 (1943), 157.

14. Bertil Romberg, *Studies in the Narrative Technique of the First-Person Novel*, pp. 43 - 46.

15. Carlos Blanco Aguinaga, "Cervantes y la picaresca: notas sobre dos tipos de realismo," *Nueva revista de filología hispánica* 2 (1957), 316.

16. Rafael Alberti, *Teatro*, pp. 9 - 12.

17. Alfonso Reyes, "Un enigma de *La Lozana andaluza*," 153.

18. Santos Sanz Villanueva in his review of my edition of *La Lozana andaluza (Soria*, April, 24, 1970).

19. Cf. Stephen Gilman, "Diálogo y estilo en la *Celestina*," *op. cit.*, pp. 461 - 69. For excellent examples of a vivid dialogue dealing with cosmetics, see *La Lozana*, ed. cit., pp. 47, 78. The meaning of

those cosmetics is explained by Felix Martí Ibáñez in "The Medico-pharmaceutical Arts of *La Celestina,*" *International Record of Medicine and General Practice Clinics* (April 1956), pp. 233 - 49.

20. In memorandum XXVIII the mail carrier refers to the vast knowledge which Lozana has gained "through experience" *(La Lozana, ed. cit.,* p. 131).

21. José Ortega y Gasset, *Meditation on Quijote,* trans. Evelyn Rugg and Diego Marín (New York: W.W. Norton, 1961), p. 157.

22. Wardropper, "La novela como retrato . . . ," 481.

23. Stephen Gilman, *op. cit.,* 464.

24. Pisanus Fraxi, *Catena Librorum Tacendorum* (New York, 1962), III, 373 - 84.

25. Luigi Foscolo Benedetto, *Le operette satiriche di Niccolò Machiavelli* (Turin, 1920), pp. V ff. Cf. Natalino Sapegno, *Compendio di Storia della Letteratura Italiana* (Florence, 1963), II, 62, 70, 72.

26. Giuseppe Toffanin, *Storia Letteraria d'Italia, "Il Cinquecento"* (Milan, 1935), p. 426.

27. Burckhardt, *op. cit.,* II, 344 - 483.

28. Graf, *op. cit.,* pp. 73 - 136.

29. Wardropper, *op. cit.,* p. 476.

30. Edwin Hood, *The Mental and Moral Philosophy of Laughter* (London, 1852), p. 11.

31. José Gómez de la Serna, *op. cit.,* p. 8.

32. Burckhardt, *op. cit.,* II, 433.

33. In *Homenaje a Dámaso Alonso* (Madrid, 1960), I, 431 - 32; also cf. Manuel Criado de Val, *De la Edad Media al Siglo de Oro, op. cit.,* p. 85.

34. Manuel Criado de Val, "Antífrasis y contaminaciones . . . ," p. 432.

35. Lincoln Rothschild, *Style in Art: The Dynamics of Art as Cultural Expression* (New York and London, 1960), p. 21.

36. Johan Huizinga, *Erasmus of Rotterdam* (London: Phaidon, 1952), p. 71.

37. Horace, *Sermons,* I, i, 24.

38. Leonard Feinberg, *The Satirist, His Temperament, Motivation, and Influence* (Ames: Iowa State University Press, 1963), pp. 18 - 41.

39. David Worcester, *The Art of Satire* (Cambridge: Harvard University Press, 1940), p. 36.

40. *Ibid.,* p. 13.

41. Francisco Márquez Villanueva, "Sebastián de Horozco y el *Lazarillo de Tormes,*" *Revista de filología española* 41 (1957), 262 - 63.

42. Spigant or Cyzico, a place in Asia Minor. In the sixteenth century the Roman Curia had as members some bishops from Eastern dioceses; these clerics must have seemed like ancient pagan priests, for wearing pompous habits. See Filippo Ferrari, *Novum Lexicon geographicum,* (Padua, 1916), p. 214; Domenico Gnoli, "La Lozana andaluza e le cortigiane . . . ," p. 166. The bishop in question must be Georgi Ridolphus, who in 1518 succeeded

Franciscus Salvinus *(La Lozana andaluza,* ed. Luisa Orioli, p. 312, note 15).

43. Mameluke: a soldier recruited from slaves converted to Islamism; he is the object of ridicule for, although he is a slave, he commands others as if he were a nobleman.

44. *The Praise of Folly,* ed. Walter Black (New York, 1942), p. 199.

45. *Tratado del alma,* . . . ed. Martín Navarro and Foster Watson (Madrid: Ediciones de la Lectura, 1916), pp. 318 - 19.

46. Serrano Poncela, *op. cit.,* pp. 118 - 19.

47. Nicasio Salvador Miguel, "En torno al *Retrato de la Lozana andaluza,*" *La estafeta literaria,* no. 373 (July, 1967), p. 12.

48. *The Anatomy of Satire* (Princeton, 1962), p. 26; cf. James Hannay, *Satire and Satirists* (London, 1854), p. 15.

49. Arthur Weston, *Latin Satirical Writing Subsequent to Juvenal* (Lancaster, 1915), p. 70.

50. Gilbert Highet, *op. cit.,* p. 236.

51. *Ibid.* p. 190.

52. See Norman Friedman, "Point of View in Fiction: The Development of a Critical Concept," in *The Novel: Modern Essays in Criticism,* p. 159.

53. Leonard Feinberg, *op. cit.,* p. 354.

54. Maurice Shroder "The Novel as a Genre," in *The Novel: Modern Essays in Criticism,* p. 46.

55. Huntington Brown, *Prose Styles* (Minneapolis: University of Minnesota Press, 1966), p. 4.

56. Menéndez Pelayo, *Orígenes,* IV,61 - 62.

57. Juan Terlingen, *Los italianismos en español desde la formación del idioma hasta principios del siglo XVII* (Amsterdam, 1943).

58. Hayward Keniston, *The Syntax of Castilian Prose: The Sixteenth Century* (Chicago, 1937).

59. Lester Beberfall, "Italian Influences on the Partitive Indefinite Construction in the *Lozana andaluza,*" 108 - 13; *idem.,* "Some Italian Influences in Delicado's La Lozana andaluza," pp. 828 - 30.

60. Menéndez Pelayo, *Orígenes,* IV, 61.

61. Juan de Valdés, *Diálogo de la lengua* (Madrid: Castalia, 1969), p. 70.

62. *Diccionario de literatura española,* . . . eds. Julián Marías and Germán Bleiberg (Madrid,1949), *s.v. refrán.* Cf. Miguel de Cervantes, *Don Quijote de la Mancha,* ed. Martín de Riquer (Barcelona, 1965) I chapter 21, p. 191.

63. These proverbs are documented in the following sources: Sebastián de Covarrubias, *Tesoro de la lengua castellana o española* . . . , ed. Martín de Riquer (Barcelona, 1943), *s.v. mayo; Ibid., s.v. asno;* Gonzalo de Correas, *Vocabulario de refranes y frases proverbiales* . . . (Madrid, 1924), p. 286; *ibid.,* pp. 38, 387, 567.

64. The significant jargon words in these passages are documented in the following sources: *Voces germanescas,* ed. John Hill (Bloomington: Indiana University Publications Humanities Series no. 21, 1949), *s.v. chiquiribaile;* Gustavo de Correas, *Vocabulario de refranes,* pp. 441, 567.

65. *Diálogo de la lengua*, ed. cit., p. 61.
66. Menéndez Pelayo, *Orígenes*, IV, 61.
67. Burckhardt, *op. cit.*, II, 473; Hernández Ortiz pays particular attention to this point (*op. cit.*, p. 111 and n. 91).
68. Segundo Serrano Poncela, "Aldonza la andaluza Lozana . . . ," p. 46; cf. Hernández, *op. cit.*, 111 ff.
69. Maurice Shroder, *op. cit.*, p. 44.
70. Ortega y Gasset, *op. cit.*, p. 181.
71. *Op. cit.*, p. 46.
72. Baltasar Gracián, *El Criticón*, in *Obras Completas*, ed. Arturo del Hoyo (Madrid, 1960), p. 908. Cf. Christo Thomas Mocas, "Aspectos lexicográficos de *La Lozana Andaluza*;" also cf. Hernández, *op. cit.*, 107 - 8, n. 82.
73. Giovanni Allegra, "Breve nota acerca del 'Ilustre señor' de la *Lozana Andaluza*," *Boletín de la real academia española* 199 (1973), 391 - 97.
74. Alfonso de Valdés, *Diálago de las cosas ocurridas en Roma*, ed. J. F. Montesinos (Madrid, 1928), p. 35.
75. John William Atkins, *Literary Criticism in Antiquity* (Cambridge, 1934), I, 53.
76. Wylie Sypher, *Four Stages of Renaissance Art* (New York, 1955), pp. 61, 76.
77. John Laird, *A Study in Realism* (Cambridge, 1920), p. 208.
78. George Burton Adams, *Civilization during the Middle Ages* (New York, 1914), p. 364.

Chapter Seven

1. F. Courtney Tarr, "Literary and Artistic Unity in the *Lazarillo de Tormes*," *Publications of the Modern Language Association of America* 42 (1927), 404 - 21.
2. *La Lozana andaluza*, ed. Antonio Vilanova, p. XXXI.
3. *La novela picaresca española*, ed. Angel Valbuena Prat (Madrid: Aguilar, 1956), p. 12.
4. George Tyler Northup, *An Introduction to Spanish Literature* (Chicago: The University of Chicago Press, 1926), p. 173; Ian Bagby, "La primera novela picaresca española," *La Torre* 18, (1970), 83 - 100.
5. Stephen Gilman, "The Death of *Lazarillo de Tormes*," *Publications of the Modern Language Association of America* 81 (1966), p. 156.
6. It is interesting to note that the allegorical gondola depicted on the title page of the Venetian edition of *Lozana* appears to be the direct model for the allegorical "Ship of the Picaresque Life" found on the frontispiece of *La pícara Justina* (1605). See *La Lozana Andaluza*, ed. Antonio Vilanova, p. LX, n. 37; Alexander Parker, *Literature and the Delinquent: A Study of the Picaresque Novel in Spain* (Edinburgh University Press, 1967), pp. XII -

XIII. With regard to the relationship of *Lozana* to *Justina*, see the introduction to my edition of *La pícara Justina* to be published soon by Castalia.

7. Carlos Blancos Aguinaga, "Cervantes y la picaresca . . . ," p. 316.

8. Pedro Penzol, *Algunos itinerarios en la literatura castellana* (Madrid, 1934), pp. 16, 17; 23 - 24. Oldřich Bělič, *Análisis estructural de textos hispánicos* (Madrid, 1969), p. 26. This point is also made by José Antonio Hernández, *op. cit.*, p. 294.

9. Claudio Guillén, "Toward a definition of the picaresque," *Actes du III Congrés de l'Association Internationale de Littérature Comparée* (The Hague, 1962), p. 259.

10. For a study of these and other characteristics of the pícaro as well as some interesting observations on the three major picaresque novels, see César Barja, *Libros y autores clásicos* (New York: Stechert, 1941), pp. 215 - 32; 313 - 25; 439 - 45; also Pedro Salinas, "El héroe literario y la novela picaresca española," *Revista de la universidad de Buenos Aires* (January - March, 1946, pp. 82 ff.)

11. *La novela picaresca española*, ed. Angel Valbuena Prat, p. 84.

12. Ian Bagby, *op. cit.*, p. 96. Cf. Peter Dunn, *Castillo Solórzano and the decline of the Spanish novel* (Oxford: Basil Blackwell, 1952), p. 115: "After *La Pícara Justina* the service of masters was eliminated from those stories in which the central character was a pícara. It is preserved to a limited extent in that the heroine, while still a girl, serves in an inn or does some kind of needlecraft . . . Her main adventures, however, are amorous conquests and 'confidence tricks,' . . ." On the topic of the female protagonist's motives for sexual promiscuity, see Rosa Pastalosky, *Henry Fielding y la tradición picaresca* (Buenos Aires: Solar, 1970), p. 79.

13. The interesting article of Ian Bagby makes this point clear (*op. cit.*, pp. 98 - 99).

14. Francisco Javier Sánchez Díez, "La novela picaresca de protagonista femenino en España durante el siglo XVII" (Ph.D. diss., University of North Carolina at Chapel Hill, 1972), p. 125; Pablo Javier Ronquillo, "Hacia una definición de la pícara del siglo XVII en España" (Ph.D. diss., Louisiana State University, 1969), p. 125.

15. Alonso de Salas Barbadillo, *La hija de Celestina*, in *La novela picaresca española*, ed. cit., p. 890 ff.

16. Alonso de Castillo Solórzano, *La niña de los embustes*, in *La novela picaresca española*, ed. Angel Valbuena Prat, pp. 1350, 1352 - 3, 1354, 1361, 1395; Alonso de Castillo Solórzano, *Las harpías de Madrid*, in *Colección selecta de antiguas novelas españolas*, ed. Emilio Cotarelo y Mori (Madrid, 1907, vol. 7, pp. 143, 145. These novels were published in 1631 and 1632.

17. Pablo Javier Ronquillo, *op. cit.*, p. 157.

18. José Antonio Hernández, *op. cit.*, p. 107.

19. *La pícara Justina*, ed. Julio Puyol y Alonso (Madrid, 1912), *Sociedad de bibliófilos madrileños*, II, 282 - 283. The erotic sentiments of other female

rogues is discussed by Pablo Javier Ronquillo, *op. cit.*, pp. 161 - 66.

20. Stuart Miller, *The Picaresque Novel* (Cleveland: Case Western Reserve Press, 1967), p. 26.

21. *Lazarillo de Tormes,* in *La novela picaresca española,* ed. Valbuena Prat, p. 90.

22. *Guzmán de Alfarache,* in *ibid.,* pp. 256 - 58.

23. Dámaso Alonso, "Escila y Caribdis de la literatura española," *Cruz y Raya* 7 (1933), 78 - 101.

24. On this point see Oldřich Bělič, "La novela picaresca española y el realismo," *Romanistica Pragensia (Acta Universitatis Carolinae, Philologica)* 2 (1961), 5 - 15.

25. The historical background of the picaresque novel is thoroughly discussed by Alberto Del Monte, *Itinerario del romanzo picaresco spagnolo* (Firenze: Sansoni, 1957) and by Oscar Borgers, "Le roman picaresque: réalisme et fiction," *Les Lettres Romanes* 14 (1960), 23 - 38; 135-48; 295 - 305.

26. See Gustave Reynier, *Le roman réaliste au dix-septième siècle* (Paris: Hachette, 1914), pp. 1 - 37; 43 - 55.

27. Erich Auerbach, *Mimesis: The Representation of Reality in Western Literature* (New York: Anchor, 1957), p. 23.

28. See Benedetto Croce, *La Spagna nella vita italiana durante la rinascenza,* pp. 164; 172; 242 - 44.

29. Ludwig Pfandl, *Historia de la literatura nacional española en la Edad de Oro* (Barcelona: Gili, 1933) pp. 291 - 320.

30. Alexander Parker, *op. cit.,* p. 25.

31. *Ibid.*

32. *Ibid.*

33. See Fonger De Haan, *An Outline of the History of the Novela Picaresca in Spain* (The Hague and New York: Nijhoff, 1903), p. 80; this aspect of the picaresque novel is documented and discussed by Joseph Ricapito, "Toward a Definition of the Picaresque: A study of the evolution of the genre together with critical and annotated bibliography of *La vida de Lazarillo de Tormes, Vida de Guzmán de Alfarache,* and *Vida del Buscón"* (Ph.D. diss., University of California, 1966), p. 525.

34. See James Stamm, "The Uses and Types of Humor in the Picaresque Novel," *Hispania* 42 (1959), 482 - 87.

35. Manuel Asensio, "El *Lazarillo de Tormes:* problemas, crítica y valoración" (Ph.D. diss., University of Pennsylvania, 1955), p. 174.

36. I was inspired to cite this dialogue by the perceptive discussion on humor which José Antonio Hernández presents in his dissertation (*op. cit.,* p. 260).

37. Américo Castro, *España en su historia* (Buenos Aires: Losada, 1948), pp. 581 - 97; see also "Un aspecto del pensar hispano-judío," *Hispania* 35 (1952), 161 - 72; Marcel Bataillon, Les nouveaux chrétienes dans l'essor du roman picaresque," *Neophilologus* 4 (1964), 283 - 98; *idem., Pícaros y picaresca,* pp. 203 - 43.

38. Américo Castro, *España en su historia,* p. 581.
39. *La picara Justina,* ed. Puyol y Alonso, II, 289.
40. See Michael Ramón, "Nueva interpretación del pícaro y de la novela picaresca española hecha a base de un estudio de las tres obras maestras del género" (Ph.D. diss., Northwestern University, 1956), pp. 89 ff.
41. José Giles y Rubio, *Origen y desarrollo de la novela picaresca* (Oviedo: Brid, 1890). This work has not been available to me; I have thus used a summary of it made by Joseph Ricapito, *op. cit.,* p. 20.

Chapter Eight

1. Joseph Gillet, *Propalladia,* III, 259 - 60.
2. Menéndez Pelayo, *Orígenes,* III, 45 - 65.
3. Benedetto Croce, *Spagna nella vita italiana* . . ., pp. 164; 172; 242; 244.
4. *Ibid.,* p. 244.
5. *La Lozana andaluza,* ed. Joaquín del Val, pp. 16 - 21.
6. Guillaume Apollinaire, *L'oeuvre du divin Aretin* (Paris, 1909 - 1923) I, 14.
7. Manzella Frontini, *La Lozana andaluza,* p. 95.

Chapter Nine

1. "Un processo a Pietro Aretino," in *Attraverso il Cinquecento,* p. 88. The immorality of the sixteenth century in Italy is also discussed by Jacob Burckhardt in *The Civilization of the Renaissance in Italy,* II, 426 - 43.
2. The interrelationship between the "immorality" of the sixteenth century and Renaissance culture is noted by Arturo Graf who remarks: "the immorality of the cinquecento, that immorality so intimately connected with Renaissance culture that if one had not existed neither would have the other" (*Attraverso il Cinquecento,* p. 88).
3. Menéndez Pelayo, *Orígenes,* IV, 57 ff.
4. In his *Storia della letteratura italiana* (Milano, 1924) II, 95 112.
5. Among others, Francesco Berni, Niccolò Franco and Anton Francesco Doni (See Arturo Graf, *op, cit.,* p. 86). For Doni's opinion of Aretino, see Luigi Russo's study "Pietro Aretino," *Belfagor* 17 (1962), p. 4. Eugenio Camerini also demonstrates the importance which the correspondence of Aretino with such noted figures as Giovanni de' Medici and Maria de' Medici has for our understanding of the man and his times (Pietro Aretino, *Le Commedie, L'Orazia,* ed. Eugenio Camerini [Milano, 1930], pp. 6 - 16).
6. See Arturo Graf, *op. cit.,* p. 119. Delicado does not hesitate to admit his quality of *hombre indocto* ("unlearned man"): *Lozana andaluza,* ed. Damiani, p. 248.
7. Francesco Flora, *Storia della letteratura italiana* (Milano: Mondadori, 1941, II, 408 - 39). Cf. also Giuliano Innamorati, "Lo stil comico di

Pietro Aretino," *Paragone* 14 (1936), 10. As for Delicado, Menéndez Pelayo (*Orígenes*, IV, 50), suggests that the Spanish prelate went to Rome in the hope of receiving some benefice which he gained with the vicarship of the Valle de Cabezuela between the years of 1529 and 1533. In *Lozana*, Delicado affirms that the publication of his work was financially motivated.

8. Details of Aretino's life are well presented in the recent biography by James Cleugh: *The Divine Aretino* (New York: Stein and Day, 1966). Also see Jefferson Butler Fletcher, *Literature of the Italian Renaissance* (New York, 1934) p. 271. As for Delicado, *Lozana* provides us with substantial evidence of his licentious life in the course of which he contracted syphilis.

9. See Arturo Graf, *op. cit.*, p. 119; cf. Bruce Wardropper, *op. cit.*, p. 476.

10. Menéndez Pelayo, *Orígenes*, IV, 57.

11. *Rassegna bibliografica della letteratura italiana* (Pisa, 1900), VII, 281.

12. Guillaume Appollinaire, *L'oeuvre de Francisco Delicado: "La Lozana andaluza"* (Paris, 1912), p. 9. The question of the authorship of *Zoppino* has also been brought forth by Gino Lanfranchi in the introduction to his edition of the *Dialogo dello Zoppino* (Milano, 1927), without proving conclusively, however, either Aretino or Delicado as the author.

13. *Le Commedie, ed. cit.*, p. 101.

14. *Ibid.*, pp. 260 - 61.

15. *I Ragionamenti*, ed. Enrico Riccardo Sampietro (Bologna, 1965), p. 75.

16. *Le Commedie, ed. cit.*, p. 124. Graf discusses at length the historicity of some of these well-known courtesans (*Attraverso il Cinquecento*, pp. 177 - 284).

17. In the introduction to the *Dialogo dello Zoppino, ed. cit.*, p. 10.

18. See *Le Commedie, ed. cit.*, pp. 268; 278; 281 - 82.

19. See, in particular, the "third day" of the *Ragionamenti, ed., cit.*, pp. 198 - 243. In the *Dialogo dello Zoppino*, note the vivid description of lascivious and gluttonous clerics (*ed. cit.*, pp. 58, 68).

20. *Attraverso il Cinquecento*, p. 129.

21. Giuseppe Toffanin, *Il Cinquecento* (Milano: Vallardi, 1929), pp. 299, 300; the quote is from James Cleugh, *op. cit.*, p. 197.

22. James Cleugh, *op. cit.*, p. 196.

23. *Pietro Aretino: Tra Rinascimento e Controriforma* (Milano, 1948), p. 269.

24. In Arturo Graf, *Attraverso il Cinquecento*, p. 73.

25. *Attraverso il Cinquecento*, p. 121.

26. Richard Garnett, "Satire," *Encyclopaedia Britannica*, v. 20, Encyclopaedia Britannica, Inc., 1948. Also, see Maurice Walsh, "Some Character Aspects of the Satirist (Pietro Aretino)," *American Imago* 18 (1961), 235 - 62.

27. In his study, "Gogol, A treatise on wit and paranoia," *Journal of the American Psychoanalytic Society*, III, no. 1 (Jan. 1955), 110 - 21.

28. *Le commedie, ed. cit.*, p. 6.

Chapter Ten

1. Theodore Shank, *The Art of Dramatic Art* (New York: Dell, 1969), p. 2.
2. Friedrich Dürrenmatt, "Preface: Problems of the Theatre," in *Four Plays: 1957 - 1962* (London: Jonathan Cape, 1964), p. 10.
3. María Rosa Lida de Malkiel, *La originalidad artística de la Celestina* (Buenos Aires, 1970), p. 326, n. 32.
4. José Gomez de la Serna, *op. cit.*, p. 8.
5. See Edward Rosenheim, *What Happens in Literature* (Chicago, 1960), p. 46.
6. This point is well discussed by José Hernández *(op. cit.,* pp. 117 - 18), in relation to the observations on realism made by Ramón Menéndez Pidal in *La epopeya castellana a través de la literatura española* (Madrid, 1959), p. 38.
7. Observations which Ian Watt makes about the modern novel, "Realism and the Novel Form," in *Approaches to the Novel,* ed. Robert Scholes (San Francisco: Chandler, 1961), p. 71.
8. *Studies in the Narrative Technique of the First Person Novel,* p. 45. Hernández (*op. cit.,* p. 72, n. 58) cites Carmelo Bonet who gives evidence that the diary technique was also used by several Spanish writers of the nineteenth century (*El realismo literario* [Buenos Aires, 1958], p. 42.)
9. Pío Baroja, *El árbol de la ciencia* (New York: Las Americas Publishing Company, n.d.) p. 283.
10. José Ortega y Gasset, *op. cit.,* p. 160.

Selected Bibliography

PRIMARY SOURCES

1. Works by Francisco Delicado

De consolatione infirmorum (On Consoling the Infirm). Rome, 1525.
Spechio vulgare per li sacerdoti che administraranno li sacramenti in ciascheduna parrochia (A Vernacular Manual for Those Priests Who will Administer the Sacraments in Each Parish). Rome, 1526?
Retrato de la Lozana andaluza (Portrait of Lozana: The Exuberant Andalusian Woman). Venice, 1528.
El modo de adoperare el legno de India occidentale (On the Use of the West Indies' Wood). Venice, 1529.
Edition of the *Tragicomedia de Calisto y Melibea (Tragicomedy of Calixtus and Melibea)*. Venice, 1531. Contains the *Introducción que muestra el Delicado a pronunciar la lengua española* (Introduction which Delicado Offers on the Pronunciation of the Spanish Language).
Edition of the *Amadís de Gaula* (Amadis of Gaul). Venice, 1533.
Edition of *Los tres libros del caballero Primaleón et Polendos su hermano* (The Three Books of the Knight Primaleón and of Polendos, His Brother). Venice, 1534.

2. Editions of *Lozana*

Retrato de la Lozana andaluza. Venice, 1528. The first known edition.
Retrato de la Lozana andaluza. Edited by the Marqués de la Fuensanta del Valle and José Sancho Rayón, Madrid, 1871. "Colección de libros españoles raros o curiosos." Volume I. A badly reproduced text of *Lozana*.
La Lozana Andaluza (La Gentille Andalouse). Edited by Alcide Bonneau. Paris, 1888. Two volumes. The first French translation of *Lozana*.
Retrato de la Lozana Andaluza. Edited by Luis de Lara. Madrid, 1899. "Colección de libros picarescos." Contains numerous textual errors.
La Lozana andaluza. Edited by Antonio Álvarez de la Villa. Paris, 1900. Erroneous text with a brief negative introduction.
La Lozana Andaluza (La Gentille Andalouse). Edited by Guillaume

Apollinaire. Paris, 1912. "Bibliothèque des curieux." The second French translation with a good introduction.
Retrato de la Lozana Andaluza. Edited by Eduardo María de Segovia. Madrid: Editorial Mundo Latino, 1916. One of the worst editions.
La Lozana andaluza. Edited by Elio Lanfranchi. Milano, 1927. A second-rate Italian translation.
La Lozana andaluza. Edited by José Gómez de la Serna. Santiago de Chile: Ediciones Ercilla, 1942. A very fine introduction but a poor text.
La Lozana Andaluza. Edited by Javier Farias. Buenos Aires: Ediciones Nuevo Romance, 1942. "Libros raros y curiosos." Volume I. Serious textual errors.
Retrato de la Lozana Andaluza. Facsimile edition of Antonio Pérez Gómez. Valencia, 1950.
La Lozana andaluza. Edited by Juan Delgado Campos. Paris, 1950. Bad text but useful glossary.
La Lozana Andaluza. Edited by Antonio Vilanova. Barcelona, 1952. Excellent introduction but an incorrect text.
La Lozana andaluza, seguida por "El coloquio de las damas" de El Aretino. Barcelona: Editorial Lorenzana, 1965. Popular edition with an inferior text and followed by Aretino's *Discourse of the Ladies.*
La Lozana Andaluza. Edited by Antonio Prieto. Barcelona: Ediciones Marte, 1967. Useless edition.
Retrato de la Lozana Andaluza. Edited by Joaquín del Val. Madrid: Ediciones Taurus, 1967. Good introduction and fair text.
La Lozana andaluza. Edited by Bruno Mario Damiani. Ph.D. diss., Johns Hopkins, 1967. A critical edition.
La Lozana andaluza. Edited by Carlos Ayala, Jaime Uyá and Francisco Fernández. Barcelona: Zeus, 1968. Useless edition.
La Lozana andaluza. Introducción, texto y notas de Bruno Mario Damiani. Madrid: Castalia, 1969. Historical introduction and annotated text with a glossary.
La Lozana andaluza. Edited by Luisa Orioli. Milano: Adelfi, 1970. Good Italian translation of the *Lozana* with a brief introduction and informative notes. Also contains an Italian translation of Delicado's *El modo de adoperare el legno de India occidentale* (On the Use of the West Indies' Wood).

SECONDARY SOURCES

ALBERTI, RAFAEL. *Teatro.* Buenos Aires, 1964. "La Lozana andaluza," pp. 8 - 82. Considers *Lozana* as a "theater of the world" and provides a dramatic rendition of the work.
ALLEGRA, GIOVANNI. "Breve nota acerca del 'Ilustre Señor' de la *Lozana Andaluza.*" *Boletín de la real academia española* 53 (1973), 391 - 97. A revealing study of the patron, Philibert of Châlons, to whom Delicado dedicates *Lozana.*

Selected Bibliography [145]

APOLLINAIRE, GUILLAUME. Introduction to *L'Oeuvre du Divin Aretin — Premiere Partie.* Paris, 1909. Affirms that Delicado is the author of the *Dialogue of Zoppino.*
ASENSIO, EUGENIO. "Juan de Valdés contra Delicado. Fondo de una polémica." In *Homenaje ofrecido a Dámaso Alonso.* Madrid, 1960. I, 101 - 13. Explains Juan de Valdes's attacks against Delicado for relying on the linguistic authority of Nebrija.
BAGBY, ALBERT IAN, JR. "*La Lozana Andaluza* vista en su perspectiva donjuanesca." *Hispanófila* 35 (1969), 19 - 25. Similarities between Lozana and the Don Juan character of the drama.
BEBERFALL, LESTER. "Italian Influences on the Partitive Indefinite Construction in the *Lozana Andaluza.*" *Italica* (1955), 108 - 13. Deals with the inconsistencies of the partitive indefinite construction in *Lozana.*
—— "Some Italian Influences in Delicado's *La Lozana Andaluza.*" *Hispania* 49 (1966), 828 - 30. In addition to the partitives as used in the *Cid* and in the *Book of Good Love,* Delicado's novel also employs the partitives common in sixteenth-century Italy.
CRIADO DE VAL, MANUEL. "Antifrasis y contaminaciones de sentido erótico en *La Lozana Andaluza.*" In *Homenaje ofrecido a Dámaso Alonso.* Madrid, 1960. I, 431 - 57. The explanation of those words which are used with an erotic meaning.
DAMIANI, BRUNO. "*La Lozana Andaluza:* Bibliografía crítica." *Boletín de la real academia española* 49 (1969), 117 - 39. A detailed account of *Lozana* criticism.
—— "Delicado and Aretino: Aspects of a Literary Profile." *Kentucky Romance Quarterly* 17 (1970), 309 - 24. A comparative analysis of novelistic art and moral purpose.
—— "*La Lozana andaluza:* tradición literaria y sentido moral." *Actas del tercer congreso internacional de hispanistas.* Mexico, 1970. pp. 241 - 48. Analysis of *Lozana* from the point of view of literary tradition (*Celestina* and the picaresque novel) and its moral didactic purpose.
—— "Some observations on Delicado's *El modo de adoperare el legno de India occidentale.*" *Quaderni-Ibero Americani* 34 (1969). An historical analysis of the treatise.
—— "Un aspecto histórico de *La Lozana andaluza,*" *Modern Language Notes* 87 (1972), 178 - 92. An historical discussion of the Roman courtesans and the "French disease."
—— Review of *La Lozana andaluza.* Edited by Luisa Orioli. *Hispanófila* 45 (1972), 87 - 89.
—— "A critical transcription of *El modo de adoperare el legno de India occidentale.*" To appear in the *Revista hispánica moderna.* Provides useful annotation to this important Renaissance treatise on the curative properties of the guayacum wood.
DÍEZ BORQUE, JOSÉ MARÍA. "Francisco Delicado, autor y personaje de *La Lozana andaluza.*" *Prohemio* 3 (1972), 455 - 66. A useful review of Delicado's dual function as author and character.

DUNN, PETER. Review of *La Lozana andaluza*. Edited by Bruno Mario Damiani. *Bulletin of Hispanic Studies* 48 (1971), 158 - 59.

EISENBERG, DANIEL. Review of *La Lozana andaluza*. Edited by Bruno Mario Damiani. *Hispanófila* 46 (1972), 78 - 80.

FOULCHÉ-DELBOSC, RAYMOND. Review of *La Lozana andaluza*. Edited by Luis de Lara. *Revue Hispanique* 6 (1899), 408.

FRONTINI, MANZELLA. *La Lozana andaluza*. Catania, 1910. Relationship with *Celestina* and the picaresque novel; Aretino's indebtedness to Delicado.

GALLINA, ANNAMARIA. "L'attività editoriale di due spagnoli a Venezia nella prima metà del '500 (Francisco Delicado y Domingo de Gaztelu)." *Studi Ispanici*. Pisa, 1962. I, 69 - 91. Shows the importance of Delicado's editorial activity.

GNOLI, DOMENICO. "*La Lozana andaluza* e le cortigiane nella Roma di Leon X." *Nuova Antologia* 7 (1931), 165 - 96. Careful study of *Lozana* and of the Roman courtesans.

HALDAS, GEORGES and HERRERA PETERE, JOSÉ. Introduction to *Amadís de Gaule* [and] *La Gentille Andalouse*. Lausanne, 1961. On the social and linguistic importance of *Lozana*.

HERNÁNDEZ, ORTIZ, JOSÉ ANTONIO. "La originalidad artística de *La Lozana andaluza*." Ph.D. diss., Yale, 1971. Excellent study of Delicado's novelistic art. Discussion of historical and literary background of *Lozana* and its relation to *Celestina* and the picaresque novel.

——— "Francisco Delicado tratadista de medicina en la Roma del Renacimiento." *Tauta* 1 (1972), 17 - 29. A popular transcription and translation of Delicado's *El modo de adoperare* . . .

JONES, JOSEPH. Review of *La Lozana andaluza*. Edited by Bruno Mario Damiani. *Hispania* 54 (1971), 968.

MALDONADO DE GUEVARA, FRANCISCO. "*La Lozana Andaluza* y el *Quijote*." *Anales Cervantinos* XI (1972), 1 - 14.

MÁRQUEZ VILLANUEVA, FRANCISCO. "El mundo converso de *La Lozana andaluza*." To appear in *Archivo Hispalense*. An inspiring study of the *converso* world of *Lozana*.

MCBRIDE, CHARLES. "A Study and Interpretation of Francisco Delicado's *Retrato de la Lozana andaluza*." Master's thesis, New York University, 1960.

MOCAS, CHRISTO THOMAS. "*Aspectos lexicográficos de la Lozana Andaluza*." Ph.D. diss., Tulane, 1954. A fine vocabulary of difficult and rare words.

MOREL FATIO, ALFRED. Review of *La Lozana andaluza*. Edited by Marqués de la Fuensanta del Valle and José Sancho Rayón. *Revue Critique* 14 (1873), 276 79.

PAGLIALUNGA DE TUMA, MERCEDES. "Erotismo y parodia social en *La Lozana andaluza*." In *La idea del cuerpo en las letras españolas* (Siglo XIII-XVII). Edited by Dinko Cvitanovic y colaboradores. Bahía Blanca: *Cuadernos del Sur*, 1973. Pp. 118 - 53. Discusses the meaning of the

Selected Bibliography

erotic element in *Lozana* in relationship to the protagonist and Renaissance society.

PIKE, RUTH. "The *Conversos* in *La Lozana Andaluza*," *Modern Language Notes* 84 (1969), 304 - 08. Brief but interesting note on the *converso* background of *Lozana*.

REAMY, MILTON GERARD. *"El Retrato de La Lozana Andaluza.* Un estudio de costumbres y precursor de la novela picaresca." Master's thesis, University of Mexico, 1946. A basic study of customs and manners, style and structure.

REYES, ALFONSO. *Obras completas.* Madrid, 1917. "La Garza Montesina." VI, 249 - 56. Delicado knew Juan del Encina and both men were acquainted with the courtesan "La Garza Montesina."

———. "Un enigma de *La Lozana Andaluza.*" In *Homenaje ofrecido a Dámaso Alonso.* Madrid, 1963. III, 151 - 54. Lozana is an erotic character, and the bedroom scene is without precedents in Spanish literature.

RUSSO, MARIA TERESA. "Una contrada di Roma sparita: appunti di topografia." *Strenna dei Romanisti* 24 (1968), 327 - 37. A few brief notes on the location of Pozzo Bianco, site of Lozana's early vicissitudes in Rome.

———. "Pozzo Bianco nella finzione letteraria e nella realtà." *L'Urbe* 24 (1962), 21 - 24. Interesting comments on the topography of Pozzo Bianco and *Lozana*.

SALVADOR, MIGUEL NICASIO. "En Torno al *Retrato de La Lozana Andaluza.*" *La Estafeta Literaria,* no. 373 (July 1967). A brief note on the use of narration and dialogue.

SERRANO PONCELA, SEGUNDO. "Aldonza la Andaluza Lozana en Roma." *Cuadernos Americanos* 122 (1962), 117 - 32. Provides a fairly detailed study of the protagonist and of the society of Renaissance Rome.

VILANOVA, ANTONIO. "Cervantes y *La Lozana Andaluza.*" *Insula,* no. 77 (May 1952). Considers *Lozana* as a work of transition between *Celestina* and the picaresque genre. Observes interesting artistic parallels between Delicado and Cervantes.

WARDROPPER, BRUCE W. "La novela como retrato: El arte de Francisco Delicado." *Nueva revista de filología hispánica* 7 (1953). 475 - 88. An excellent study of Delicado's novelistic technique.

Index

Abenámar, 34
Abiram, 29
Aeschines, 126n10
Agrippa, 112
Aguilaret, 82-83
Aguilocho, Pedro, 34
Alberti, Rafael, 55
Aldonza, Lozana's birthname, 18
Alemán, Mateo, 98
Alexander VI, Pope (Rodrigo Borja), 14, 47, 58
Alfonso el Sabio (the Learned - X of Castile), 125n9
Alfonso of Aragon, 14
Allegra, Giovanni, 88
Alvigia (In *La Cortigiana*), 113
Amadís de Gaula. *See* Delicado, Francisco
Ambron family, 60
Aminthas (In *Thebaida*), 38
Anales históricos de la medicina (Historical Annals of Medicine). *See* Chinchilla, Anastasio
Andrea, Maestro (In *La Cortigiana*), 112, 117
Angioletta of Naples, The courtesan (In *La Cortigiana*), 113
"Antiphrases and Contaminations of Erotic Meaning in *Lozana*." *See* Criado de Val, Manuel
Antonio (In *Ragionamenti*), 113
Apitius, Marcus, 28
Apollinaire, Guillaume, 109, 111
Apuleius, 27, 86
Aquinas, Saint Thomas, 115
Arbol de la ciencia, El (The Tree of Knowledge). *See* Baroja, Pío

Aretino, Pietro, 21-22, 108-109, 110-18, 139n5
WORKS:
Dialogo dello Zoppino (Dialogue of Zoppino), 111
Puttana errante (Wandering Harlot), 111
Ragionamenti (Discussions), 21, 108-109, 111, 112-13, 114, 118
Cortigiana, La (The Courtesan), 111-12, 113, 114, 117, 118
Talanta, The, 112, 113, 114
Prose Sacre (Sacred Prose), 114-15, 118
Vita di San Tommaso d'Aquino (Life of Saint Thomas Aquinas), 115
Ariosto, Ludovico, 41
Aristophanes, 64
Aristotle, 25-26, 31, 62, 78, 90, 133n5
Armellini, Mariano: *Census*, 49, 51
Arthemis (In *Serafina*), 38
Ascarelli family, 60
Ashbee, Henry Spencer, 71
Catena Librorum Tacendorum (Bibliography of Forbidden Books), 71
Astruc, Jean, 107, 108; *De morbis venereis (On Venereal Pustules)*, 107, 108
Auerbach, Erich, 98
Aviñonesa, Madam, The courtesan (In *Lozana*), 51

Bagby, Albert Ian, 24
Balaam, 29
Ballad of Abenámar, 34
Ballads of the Cid, 34
Banchi. *See* Bancos District

[149]

Bancos, District of Rome, 95, 112, 113
Bandello, Matteo, 52
Barbosa, Arias, 51
Baroja, Pío, 121; *El árbol de la ciencia (The Tree of Knowledge)*, 121
Bataillon, Marcel, 101
Beatrice, The courtesan (In *La Cortigiana*), 113
Beatrice Yspana (In Armellini's *Census*), 49
Beatriz de Baeza (In *Lozana*), 49, 57, 59, 67-68; *See also* Beatrice Yspana
Beberfall, Lester, 23, 82
Bělič, Oldřich, 93
Bible, The, 28-29, 30, 43, 76, 78, 105, 115
Bibliography of Forbidden Books, 71
Bonneau, Alcide, 22, 111
Book of Good Love, 22, 29-31
Borgia. *See* Borja, Rodrigo
Borgo, 113
Borja, Rodrigo (Pope Alexander VI), 14, 49, 58
Borromeo, Federico, Cardinal, 60
Boscán, Juan, 15-16
Bracciolini, Poggio, 34, 105-106
Brown, Huntington, 78
bubas. *See* syphilis
Burcado, Giovanni, 48
Burckhardt, Jacob, 71, 72, 85
Burgos, 35

Cáceres, 14
Caesar, Julius, 112
Calabraga, 19
Calisto, 36
Calixtus III, Pope, 47
Camerini, Eugenio, 139n5
Camillus (In *Lozana*), 84
Campidolio (In *Lozana*), 68
Campo de Flor, 49, 51, 68
Cancionero. *See* Horozco, Sebastián de
Cancionero de obras de burlas provocantes a risa (Songbook of Burlesque Works that Provoke Laughter), 38
Cárcel de amor (Prison of Love) 14, 15, 36, *See also* Delicado, Francisco
Carrión, Count of, 34
Cary, Joyce, 45
Casalduero, Joaquín, 62
Castile, 33

Castillo Solórzano, Alonso de, 96
Castro, Américo, 101, 133n7; "Algunos temas de la *Celestina,*" 133n7
Catena Librorum Tacendorum (Bibliography of Forbidden Books). *See* Ashbee, Henry Spencer
Ceca, 50
Celestina, 16, 23, 35, 36, 38, 68, 92, 128n46
Celestine II, Pope, 35
Celidonia, The courtesan (In *Lozana*), 100
Census. *See* Armellini, Mariano
Centeno, Hernán, 34
Cervantes Saavedra, Miguel de, 23, 46, 99, 117; *Quijote,* 46
Charles V, Holy Roman Emperor, 105
Charles VIII, King of France, 53
Chinchilla, Anastasio, 107; *Anales históricos de la medicina (Historical Annals of Medicine)*, 107
Cicero, Marcus Tullius, 26
Cid, El. *See* "Romancero del Cid"
"civil register". *See* "jure cevil"
Clarina, The courtesan (In *Lozana*), 51, 81, 85
Claros varones de Castilla (Illustrious Men of Castile), 33-34
Clement VII, Pope, 105, 107
Comedia Serafina, 28, 38
Collosseum, 50, 68, 112
Comedia Soldadesca, 37
Comedia Tinelaria, 37
comedias a noticia, 37
Concilio de los galanes y cortesanas de Roma, invocado por Cupido, 37
conversos, 13, 18-19, 55-61, 101, 119-20, 131n43
Coplas de Fajardo (Couplets of Fajardo), 38
Corbacho o Reprobación del amor mundano ("Whip" or *Reprobation of Mundane Love),* 22, 31-33
Corcos family, 60
Cordova, 13, 18, 34, 75
Coridón (In *Lozana*), 78-79, 80, 100
Coriolano (In *Dialogue of the Language*), 83
Cornwall, 100

Index

Corominas, 30
Cortigiana, La (The Courtesan). See Aretino, Pietro
Council of the Lovers and Courtesans of Rome, Called by Cupid, 37
Counter Reformation, 115
Couplets of Fajardo, 38
Criado de Val, Manuel, 23, 73, 133n7; "Antífrasis y contaminaciones de sentido erótico en *La Lozana andaluza*" ("Antiphrases and Contaminations of Erotic Meaning in *Lozana*"), 73, *De la Edad Media Siglo de Oro,* 133n7
cristianos viejos, 101
Croce, Benedetto, 36, 107-108
cuaderno, 37
Cuestión de amor (Question of Love), 15, 36-37, 38
Cupid, 27, 37
Cyzico. See Spigant

Dathan, 29
De consolatione infirmorum (On Consoling the Infirm). See Delicado, Francisco
De epidemia quam Itali morbum gallicum vocant (On the Sickness Which the Italians Call Gallic Disease). See Leonicemus, Nicolaus
Delicado, Francisco: birth, 13; and Aretino, 110-117; as author, 40-42; as character in *Lozana,* 20, 21, 36, 40-46, 65-66, 77; editorial activity, 16-17; education, 13; family, 13; influence on Aretino and other writers, 108-109; knowledge of Jewish and converso customs, 60; original surname, 13; novelistic art, 30, 39, 52, 63-91; physical description, 103; in Rome, 13; in Venice, 15-16; vicar of Martos, 13; vicar of Valle de Cabezuela, 14; victim of syphilis, 52, 104
WORKS:

Amadís de Gaula (Amadís of Gaul), edition of, 14, 16
Cárcel de amor (Prison of Love), edition of, 14, 15, 36
De consolatione infirmorum (On Consoling the Infirm), 14, 54, 88
El modo de adoperare el legno de India occidentale (On the Use of the West Indies' Wood, 14, 16, 28, 53, 54, 103-109
"*Introducción que muestra el Delicado a pronunciar la lengua española*" ("Introduction Which Delicado Offers on the Pronunciation of the Spanish Language"), 16 17
Los tres libros del caballero Primaleón et Polendos su hermano (The Three Books of the Knight Primaleón and of Polendos, His Brother), edition of, 16
Retrato de la Lozana andaluza (Portrait of Lozana: The Exuberant Andalusian Woman), 15, 16, 18-102, 111-21
Spechio vulgare per li sacerdoti che administraranno li sacramenti in ciascheduna parrochia (A Vernacular Manual for Those Priests Who Will Administer the Sacraments in Each Parish), 15
Tragicomedia de Calisto y Melibea (Tragicomedy of Calixtus and Melibea), known as *Celestina,* edition of, 16, 17
De morbis venereis (On Venereal Pustules). See Astruc, Jean
Demosthenes, 26
De pudendraga sive morbo gallico (On Genital or Venereal Disease). See Torella, Gaspar
De re coquinaria (On Culinary Art), 28
De Sanctis, Francesco, 110, 116
Desperaendios, Juan, 34-35
De voluptatibus (On Pleasures), 36
Diálogo de la lengua (Dialogue of the Language). See Valdés, Juan de
Dialogo dello Zoppino (Dialogue of Zoppino). See Aretino, Pietro
Diario. See Infessura, Esteban
Didot, Firmin and Brothers (Publishers), 107; *Nouvelle biographie générale (New General Biography),* 107
Díez Borque, José María, 45-46
Diomedes (In *Lozana),* 18, 41, 52, 66, 80, 92, 93, 96

Divicia, The courtesan (In *Lozana*), 48, 53, 85, 104
Domínguez Bordona, Jesús, 33
Don Juan, 24, 34
Dorotea (In the novel of Castillo Solórzano), 96
Dunn, Peter, 137n12
Dürrenmatt, Friedrich, 119

Elena (In *La hija de la Celestina*), 95-96
El modo de adoperare el legno de India occidentale (On the Use of the West Indies' Wood). See Delicado, Francisco
Encina, Juan del, 14
Enrique IV, King of Castile and León, 33
Erasmus, Desiderius, 23, 24, 73, 76; *Praise of Folly*, 24, 76; *Handbook of the Christian Soldier*, 76
Este, Isabella d' (Marchioness of Mantua), 14
Expulsion Edict of 1492, 13, 56, 58, 98

Facetiae (Humorous Pleasantries), 34
Falillo (In *Lozana*), 57, 59
Farinelli, Arturo, 111
Feinberg, Leonard, 74, 78
Felisel (In *Cuestión de amor*), 36
Ferdinand, King (II of Aragon - V of Castile; "The Catholic"), 56, 57, 58
Fernández de Oviedo, Gonzalo, 103, 105; *Historia general y natural de las Indias (General and Natural History of the Indies)*, 105
Ferrara, 34
Flamiano (In *Cuestión de amor*), 36
Franco, Niccolò, 52
Franquila (In *Thebaida*), 38
Fraxi, Pisanus *(pseud.)* See Ashbee, Henry Spencer
"French affliction." *See* syphilis
"French disease." *See* syphilis
Frontini, Manzella, 109
Fuensanta del Valle, Marqués de la, 111
Fueter, Edward, 33

"Gallic disease." *See* syphilis
"Gallic pustules." *See* syphilis
Garnett, Richard, 117
Garza Montesina, La, The courtesan (In *Lozana*), 51

Gayangos, Paścual de, 21, 124
Generaciones y Semblanzas, 33
Generations and Sketches, 33
Gillet, Joseph, 49, 128n56
Gilman, Stephen, 92
Gnoli, Domenico, 50, 51
Gogol, Nikolai Vasilievich, 117
Golden Ass, The, 27-28
Gómez de la Serna, José, 22
Gomorrah, 29, 43
Gonnella, Pietro, 34
González Muela, Joaquín, 126-27n28
Graf, Arturo, 52, 71, 110, 114, 116-17, 139n2
grillimón, 53-54; *see also* syphilis
guayacán. See guaiacum wood
guayaco. See guaiacum wood
guaiacum wood, 15, 54-55, 103-109
guglia, La, 112
Guicciardini, Francesco, 71
Guzmán, Alfonso Enrique de, 49
Guzmán de Alfarache, 22, 45-46, 97, 98

Hamilton, Clayton, 40
Handbook of the Christian Soldier. *See* Erasmus, Desiderius
Hebrew Wisdom literature, 55
Hernández, Marina (In *Lozana*), 57
Hernández, Morejón Antonio, 54, 107; *Historia bibliográfica de la medicina española (Bibliographical History of Spanish Medicine)*, 54 107
Hernández Ortiz, José Antonio, 24, 63, 64, 125-26n9
Highet, Gilbert, 77
Hija de la Celestina, La, (The Daughter of Celestina). See Salas Barbadillo, Alonso de
Historia bibliográfica de la medicina española. See Hernández Morejón, Antonio
Historia general y natural de las Indias (General and Natural History of the Indies). See Fernández de Oviedo, Gonzalo
History of Spanish and Portuguese Literature, 21
Hood, Edwin, 72
Horace, 74, 77
Hornachuelos, "Newly married man from," 35

Index

Horozco, Sebastián de, 54; *Cancionero,* 54
Hugh of Bourbon, 88
"Humanity of Christ," 114
Humorous Pleasantries, 34

Illustrious Men of Castile, 33-34
Imperia, The courtesan (In *La Cortigiana*), 113
Imperia, The courtesan (In *Lozana*), 84
Indies, The disease from the. *See* syphilis.
Infessura, Esteban, 48; *Diario,* 48
Inquisition, 13, 56, 58
Introducción que muestra el Delicado a pronunciar la lengua española ("Introduction Which Delicado Offers on the Pronunciation of the Spanish Language"). *See.* Delicado, Francisco
Isabella, Queen of Castile, "The Catholic," 56, 58
Isis, 28

Jacomina (In *Lozana*), 44, 75
Jaén, 13
Jerez, 18
Jews: dietary laws, 57; distinguished Spanish Jews of Rome, 60; exile from Spain, 14; exodus to Italy, 14, 47; expulsion of non-converted Jews, 56; the *Judería* of Rome, 59; studies on the, 131n43; and synagogues of Rome, 58, 60; wearing distinguishing badge, 59, 67-68
Joseph, ha Cohen, 60; *Valley of Tears,* 60
Julius II, Pope, 43
"jure cevil" ("civil law," "civil register"), 64
Justina, The country jilt (In *La pícara Justina*), 96, 101
Juvenal, 26, 77

Kanzer, Marc, 117
Keniston, Hayward, 82
Kierkegaard, Sören Aabye, 121; *Skyldig - Ikke Skyldig (Guilty - Not Guilty),* 121

Laird, John, 90
Lampillas, Xavier Francisco, 107; *Saggio Storico - Apologetico della Letteratura Spagnuola (Historico - Apologetic Essay of Spanish Literature),* 107
Lanfranchi, Gino, 114
Lara, Luis de, 21
Lazarillo (legendary figure), 34
Lazarillo de Tormes, 22, 75, 92, 93, 94, 97, 101
Leghorn, 18, 93
Leo X, Pope, 49, 65
Leonicemus, Nicolaus, 106
De epidemia quam Itali morbum gallicum vocant (On the Sickness Which the Italians call Gallic Disease), 106
Libro de Buen Amor (Book of Good Love), 22, 29-31
Lipari, 20, 85, 96
López de Cortegana, Diego, 27, 28
López de Úbeda, Francisco, 101; *La pícara Justina (Justina: The Country Jilt),* 54, 101, 136-137n6
Lorenzina, The courtesan (In *La Cortigiana*), 113
Lozana, 18-21, 24, 28, 33, 34, 40, 42-45, 49-52, 56-59, 63, 66, 67-73, 74, 75, 76, 77, 78, 79, 80, 81, 84-85, 86, 87, 88, 89, 90-91, 92, 93, 94, 95, 96, 100, 101, 102, 111, 113, 120
Lubbock, Percy, 45
Lucan, 27
Lucretia, Tomb of, 69

McGrady, Donald, 45
mace bearer (In *Lozana*), 19, 96
Maco, Messer (In *La Cortigiana*), 112, 117
Machiavelli, Niccolò, 71
mail carrier (In *Lozana*), 19, 48, 96, 113
mal de Francia. See syphilis
mal de Nápoles. See syphilis
mal del greñimón. See syphilis
mal francés. See syphilis
mal francorum. See syphilis
mala franzos. See syphilis
mal incurable. See syphilis
Malkiel, María Rosa Lida de, 119
mamotreto (As literary device), 20, 64-66, 121

Marciana, Library of Venice, 106
Marcio (In *Dialogue of the Language*), 84
Maricastaña, 35
Márquez Villanueva, Francisco, 56, 58, 75, 131n43, 132n60
Marseilles, 18
Martial, 27
Martínez de Toledo, Alfonso, Archpriest of Talavera, 22, 31-33
Mártir, Peter, 53
Martos, 13, 15
Mazarine, Library of Paris, 106
Medici (de') Lorenzo, il Magnifico, 133n7; *Trionfo di Bacco e Arianna*, 133n7
Medina del Campo, 101
Melibea, 36
memorial, 36
Mencia (In *Lozana*), 49
Menéndez Pelayo, Marcelino, 22, 23, 39, 55, 84, 107, 109, 110, 111, 116, 119, 128n46
Menzia Aloysia, Madonna (In Armellini's *Census*), 49
Merlín, 34
Metamorphoses. See *Golden Ass, The*
Mocas, Christo Thomas, 23
Montoro, Antón de, 34
morbus gallicus. See syphilis
Moses, 29

Nagona. See Plaza Navona
Nanna (In *Ragionamenti*), 113
Naples, 36, 53
Navagero, Andrea, 15, 105
"Neapolitan disease." See syphilis
Neapolitan Woman (Rampí's mother), 19, 50, 84, 97
Nebrija, Antonio de, 13
New Christians. See "conversos"
Nigroponte, 93
Nouvelle biographie générale (New General Biography). See Didot

"*old christians.*" See "cristianos viejos"
On Pleasures, 36
Ortega y Gasset, José, 69, 86, 121
Ovidian (concept of love), 80

Pantheon, 69, 112

Panza, Sancho, 83
Papiense, Juan Bautista, 103
Paracelsus *(pseud.)*, 106
Parione, 49
Paris, 106
Parker, Alexander, 99
Penacho, 44
Penzol, Pedro, 93
Pérez de Guzmán, Fernán, 33
Persius, 26
Petrarch, 60
Petrocchi, Giorgio, 115
Petronius, Arbiter: *Satyricon*, 98
Philibert of Chalôns, 88
Piazza Navona. See Plaza Navona
Pícara Justina, La (Justina: The Country Jilt). See López de Ubeda, Francisco
Pike, Ruth, 57
Pippa (Nanna's daughter in *La Cortigiana*), 113
Psyche (Tale of Cupid and Psyche), 27
Pius V, Pope, 48
Plato, 27, 63, 90
"Plays about real things," 37
Plaza Nagona. See Plaza Navona
Plaza Navona, 43, 49, 51, 56, 69
Plaza Redonda, 69
Polidora (In *Lozana*), 80, 100
Ponte Sisto, 49-51, 113
Ponzio (In *The Talanta*), 112
Porfirio, 27
Pozo Blanco, 18, 49-51, 56, 57.
Pozzo Bianco. See Pozo Blanco
Praise of Folly, 24
Pratica Copiosa in Arte Chirurgica (Complete Manual of Surgical Arts). See Vigo, Juan de
Primaleón. See Delicado, Francisco
Prieto, Antonio, 46
Prison of Love, 14, 15, 36
Propaladia. See Torres Naharro, Bartolomé de
Prose Sacre (Sacred Prose). See Aretino, Pietro
Puerto, Bartolomé del, 34
Pulgar, Hernando del, 33-34
Puttana Errante (Wandering Harlot). See Aretino, Pietro

Question of Love, 15, 36-37, 38

Index

Quevedo, Francisco de, 98, 99
Quijote. See Cervantes, Saavedra, Miguel de

Ragionamenti (Discussions). See Aretino, Pietro
Rampín (In *Lozana*), 19, 21, 34, 38, 41-43, 45, 47-48, 50-51, 52, 59, 60, 68-69, 70, 72, 73, 74, 75, 76, 77, 80, 84, 85, 96-97, 102, 111-12, 117, 120
Rapallo, 105
Remus, 69
"Renaissance spirit," 63, 133n7
Reyes, Alfonso, 52, 67, 125n18
Robusto, 29
Rodamus (River), 103
Rodriguillo, 68
Romance de Abenámar (Ballad of Abenámar), 37
Romancero del Cid (Ballads of the Cid), 34
Romberg, Bertil, 41, 121
Rome, sack of, 15, 36, 44, 46, 65, 88, 89-90, 99, 105, 115-16
Romulus, 69
Ropero, 56
Rota, Julio Marciano, 103
Roth, Cecil, 58
Rothschild, Lincoln, 73
Russo, Maria Teresa, 50
Ruiz, Juan, Archpriest of Hita, 22, 30-31

Sabio, Nicolini da, 15
Sacchetti, Franco, 34
Sacchi, Bartolomé dei, 36
Saggio Storico-Apologetico della Letteratura Spagnuola (Historico-Apologetic Essay of Spanish Literature). See Lampillas, Xavier Francisco
Sagüeso (In *Lozana*), 100
Saint James, 103
Saint James (Hospital of), 14
Saint Martha, 103
Saint Peter's Church, 112, 113
Salas Barbadillo, Alonso de, 96; *La hija de la Celestina (The Daughter of Celestina)*, 95-96
Salvador Miguel, Nicasio, 76, 125n24
San Pedro, Diego de, 36, 46
Sancho Rayón, José, 111

Santa Maria Vallicella, Church of, 50
Santiago. *See* Saint James
santo grillimón, 54; *see also* syphilis
Saracín (In *Lozana*), 75
Satyricon. See Petronius, Arbiter
Segorbesa, 83
Seneca, 26, 56, 95, 125n9
Senno, Domingo, 103
Serrano Poncela, Segundo, 23, 51, 76
Setemzonéis, 69
Seville, 18, 27
Sevillian Composition of 1510, 57
Sevillian Woman, a shirtmaker (In *Lozana*), 18
Shipley, Joseph: *Dictionary of World Literature*, 133n5
Shroder, Maurice, 86
Silvio (In *Lozana*), 44-45, 46
Skyldig - Ikke Skyldig (Guilty - Not Guilty). See Kierkegaard, Sören Aabye
Socrates, 63
Sodom, 29, 43
Soldadesca. See Torres Naharro, Bartolomé de
Solórzano, Castillo, 96
Songbook of Burlesque Works that Provoke Laughter, 38
Song of Gómez Arias, 35
Sorolla, Mossén (In *Lozana*), 83
"Spanish disease." See syphilis
Spechio vulgare per li sacerdoti che administraranno li sacramenti in ciascheduna parrochia (A Vernacular Manual for Those Priests Who Will Administer the Sacraments in Each Parish. See Delicado, Francisco
Spigant, 75, 134-135n42
Sumario de la Medicina ... con un tratado sobre las pestíferas bubas (Summary of Medicine ... With a Treatise on the Pestiferous Pustules). See Villalobos (Dr.)
syphilis, 15, 52-55, 77, 88, 89, 103-109, 119

Talanta, The. See Aretino, Pietro
tarasca, 103
Tasso, Torquato, 14
Teresa de Córdoba (In *Lozana*), 57-58
Terlingen, John, 82

Teresa de Manzanares, 96
Thebaida, 38
"tierra de Cornualla", 100
Tinelaria. See Torres Naharro, Bartolomé de
Tirso de Molina *(pseud.),* 24
Toffanin, Giuseppe, 115
Torella, Gaspar, 106; *De pudendraga sive morbo gallico (On Genital or Venereal Disease),* 106
Torquemada, Juan de, 14
Torre de Nona, 112
Torres Naharro, Bartolomé de, 14, 37-38, 79, 114 *Propaladia* ("First Fruits of Pallas"), 37, 49; *Soldadesca,* 79, 114; *Tinelaria,* 37, 79, 114;
Tragicomedia de Calisto y Melibea (Tragicomedy of Calixtus and Melibea), 16, 17, 35-36, 92; *see also* Delicado, Francisco
Trecentonovelle (Three Hundred Short Stories), 34
Trigo, The Jew (In *Lozana),* 19, 51, 59-60, 94
Trissino, Gian Giorgio, 17

Urdemalas, Pedro de, 34
Usque, Solomon, 60

Val, Joaquín del, 108
Valdés, (In *Dialogue of the Language),* 83, 84
Valdés, Alfonso de, 52, 89
Valdés, Juan de, 17, 37, 83; *Diálogo de la lengua (Dialogue of the Language),* 17, 83, 84
Valencia, 38
Valle de Cabezuela, 14
Valley of Tears. See Joseph ha Cohen
Velázquez, 46
Vecellio, Cesare, 51
Venice, 15-16, 21, 89, 99, 106, 115
Vergolo, Messer (In *The Talanta),* 112
Victoria (In *Lozana),* 44
Vigo, Juan de, 106; *Pratica Copiosa in Arte Chirurgica (Complete Manual of Surgical Arts),* 106
Vilanova, Antonio, 23, 125n24
Villalobos (Dr.), 106; *Sumario de la medicina ... Con un tratado sobre las pestíferas bubas (Summary of Medicine ... With a Treatise on the Pestiferous Pustules),* 106
Vinci, Leonardo da, 106
Vita di San Tommaso d'Aquino (Life of Saint Thomas Aquinas). See Aretino, Pietro
Vives, Juan Luis, 37, 76
Voltaire (François-Marie Arouet), 117

waiter (In *Lozana),* 19
Wandering Jew, The, 35
Wardropper, Bruce, 23, 43, 124n18
Warren, Austin, 62
"Watchtower on Human Life." *See Guzmán de Alfarache,* 98
Weiner, Jack, 54
Wellek, René, 62
Whinnom, Keith, 128-29n58
Wolf, Ferdinand, 21, 124n2
Worcester, David, 74

Xuárex, Fernán, 53

Zaragoza, Jewish Woman of, 35